About the Author

Dr. Donald R. Burleson is a mathematician, retired college professor, author of many books and journal articles, and a certified Field Investigator for MUFON, the Mutual UFO Network, in which he also serves as a consultant, research specialist, certified field investigator, and State Director for New Mexico. He has also done research for CUFOS, the J. Allen Hynek Center for UFO Studies, and has appeared on *Good Morning America*, *Nightline*, Fox, the History Channel, and the Discovery Channel in connection with his work in the field of UFO studies. He once held a Top Secret clearance in U. S. Air Force intelligence, and holds master's degrees in both mathematics and English and a Ph.D. in English literature. Dr. Burleson and his wife Mollie live in Roswell, New Mexico.

Some other books by Donald R. Burleson

Field of UFO studies:

The Golden Age of UFOs
UFOs and the Murder of Marilyn Monroe

Literary Criticism:

Begging to Differ: Deconstructionist Readings
Lovecraft: Disturbing the Universe
H. P. Lovecraft: A Critical Study

Novels:

Flute Song (The Roswell Crewman)
Arroyo
A Roswell Christmas Carol

Collections of Short Stories:

Beyond the Lamplight
Four Shadowings
Lemon Drops and Other Horrors

UFO Secrecy and the Fall of J. Robert Oppenheimer

by

Donald R. Burleson, PhD.

BLACK MESA PRESS

Roswell, New Mexico
www.blackmesapress.com

Copyright © 2009 Donald R. Burleson
Published by

Black Mesa Press
P.O. Box 583
Roswell, NM 88202-0583
www.blackmesapress.com

All rights reserved. Except for the inclusion of brief quotations in a review, no part of this book may be reproduced or transmitted in any form or by any electronic or mechanical means whatever, including photocopying, audio or video recording, or by any information storage and retrieval system without prior written permission of the author or publisher. For information, please write to the above address, or contact the author by telephone at 575-622-0855 or by email at donaldrburleson@yahoo.com .

Cover/backmatter art Copyright © 2009 Mollie L. Burleson. All rights reserved.

Library of Congress Control Number:
2008906939

ISBN 0-9649580-6-6

FIRST EDITION

Printed in the United States of America by

Network Printers / Pronto Print Inc.
1010 S. 70th Street
Milwaukee, Wisconsin 53214

Voor OPJE,
natuurlijk.

Acknowledgments

I wish to thank Mark Rodeghier of CUFOS, the J. Allen Hynek Center for UFO Studies in Chicago, and the rest of the editorial board at *IUR*, the *International UFO Reporter*, for permission to quote rather freely, in the "Coda" section here, from my article "UFO Secrecy and the Law" in the Winter 2003-4 issue.

I also wish to acknowledge that my two-part article "Oppenheimer and UFOs" appeared in the June 2005 and July 2005 issues of the *MUFON UFO Journal*, published by the Mutual UFO Network; that article in effect was my dress rehearsal for this book, and was the first time it had been suggested that Dr. Oppenheimer lost his clearance due, at least in part, to his involvement in UFO-related matters. This book explores the subject in considerably more detail than was feasible in the *Journal*.

I wish to thank friends and colleagues who have cheered me on in this project, as well as the Mathematics Department at Eastern New Mexico University / Roswell (I am retired from full-time teaching but still teach part-time) for not minding my taking a summer off to work on this book.

I wish to thank my wonderful wife Mollie for doing the cover sketch of Oppie and the drawing at the end of the book, and for her love, patience, and understanding; when a book is being born, the birth is never easy.

Finally, I wish to thank J. Robert Oppenheimer for having lived, for having served his science and his country, and for having provided inspiration to so many people during his remarkable life.

Donald R. Burleson, Ph.D.
Roswell, New Mexico

Contents

Prelude: My Hypothesis 1

1. J. Robert Oppenheimer: Before the Fall 4
2. The Dark World of UFO Secrecy 19
3. Oppenheimer and UFO Crash Retrieval Activities 23
4. MJ-12: Truman's Insiders 34
5. Eisenhower Drops his own Bomb 44
6. The AEC Hearing: A Travesty in Several Acts 52
7. Aftermath: Oppenheimer Out of the Loop—What's Wrong with this Picture? 71

Coda: Some Awkward Facts about Government Secrecy 86

References and Suggested Reading

Blow, blow, thou winter wind.
Thou art not so unkind
As man's ingratitude . . . .
—Shakespeare

Mitt der Dummheit kämpfen Götter
selbst vergebens.
—Schiller

Rien ne pèse tant qu'un secret.
— La Fontaine

Prelude:
My Hypothesis

In writing about an enormously important historical figure like the incomparable J. Robert Oppenheimer, with strong reference to the field of UFO studies, I am not unaware that people attracted to the study of history in many cases are not terribly impressed with the subject of unidentified flying objects, and people attracted to reading in the field of UFO studies in many cases find themselves perusing much that is mystical and bizarre rather than crisply historical. It is my hope, however, in writing about a topic that straddles both realms, not to disenchant both groups, but rather to shed some new light on the concerns dear to both.

Tragically, after Oppenheimer had become a uniquely fascinating national hero following the successful development, under his directorship, of the world's first atomic bomb, and even after the government of the United States continually sought and received his guidance on matters of nuclear energy during the post-war years, they turned on him like a pack of dogs when President Eisenhower suspended his security clearance in December 1953 and when the Atomic Energy Commission, in the hearings of April-May 1954, refused to reinstate his clearance, thus effectively barring him from ever working in the field again. While the reasons formally given for this outrage had to do essentially with Oppenheimer's pre-war political leanings, together with his post-war reservations (shared by many prominent scientists) about the development of the hydrogen bomb, I will argue here that a broader understanding of the real reasons why he was banished from public service requires awareness of far other matters– matters that may sound like conspiracy theory to some, though I will endeavor to show here that they are far from being fanciful or groundless.

The Hypothesis

That J. Robert Oppenheimer was involved, by the direction of at least one American president, in at least two highly secret UFO crash retrieval operations, and that the real reasons for the discontinuance of his security clearance had a great deal to do with the desire of some government officials to take him 'out of the loop' with regard to finding out any more about the government's involvement in UFO retrievals than he already knew, given the reservations already held, by some, about his political leanings and temperament.

A hypothesis of course is just this: a well-considered theory that, if true, would better explain the known facts than other hypotheses do. I will argue here, I believe with considerable justification, that Oppenheimer's downfall is substantially better understood in light of the hypothesis I have stated. (I am a professional mathematician, and I do not take the logical and evidential support of hypotheses lightly.) Simply put, he was shafted by the government he had so admirably served, and they gave less than truthful reasons for their treatment of him.

Albert Einstein may have made the best remark of all, about Oppenheimer. When told that Oppenheimer was planning to undergo hearings to attempt to win back his security clearance rather than just walking away and calling his inquisitors idiots, Einstein remarked: "The trouble with Oppenheimer is that he loves a woman who doesn't love him– the United States government" (Isaacson, 532).

Come along with me and see just how right Einstein was about that.

1.
J. Robert Oppenheimer: Before the Fall

  Ingratitude is one of the ugliest of human traits. And when it takes the collective form of a government's being so ungrateful to a national hero as to dump on him the way the United States government dumped on Dr. J. Robert Oppenheimer, ingratitude is uglier than ever.
  But, as we shall see, the matter isn't so simple as all that. The reasons why Oppenheimer took the fall are dark and complex. Nothing can fully justify what was done to him, but it may be possible to get at an improved understanding of *why* it was done to him. Seen in that light, his fate, however appallingly unfair, may take on a sort of inevitability, given the way governments work.
  But I'm getting ahead of my story. First, let's meet Julius Robert Oppenheimer.
  Born on 22 April 1904 in New York, he was almost the stereotype of a bookishly precocious child and acquired an early interest in science due to a high school teacher of chemistry and physics who took him under wing. After he graduated he spent considerable time in the mountainous regions of northern New Mexico, foreshadowing the selection, two decades later, of Los Alamos as the site where he would spearhead the development of the world's first atomic bomb.

Oppenheimer entered Harvard in 1922, where he took overloads of courses and read voraciously (not just in science, but in literature and classical languages as well– throughout his life he would be a true Renaissance man– and graduated in only three years with a bachelor's degree in chemistry. That same year (1925) he went to England and entered Christ College, Cambridge University, where he studied initially with J. J. Thomson, the Nobel-laureate theoretical physicist who first demonstrated the existence of electrons.

It was through reading the professional journals, including *Zeitschrift für Physik,* that Oppenheimer encountered Heisenberg's now famous paper introducing the world to the newly discovered field of quantum mechanics. Like Einstein, Oppenheimer at first did not warm to quantum mechanics too quickly, resenting its apparent ambiguities and feeling uncomfortable with the seeming departure of its counterintuitive logic from classical patterns of thought.

However, he would soon find himself in the midst of luminaries in the field of quantum physics: Rutherford, Niels Bohr, Paul Dirac, and others. In 1926 Oppenheimer published his first two research papers, both in the area of quantum mechanics (specifically, molecular spectra and transition to continuous states in hydrogenic atoms), and it was because of these papers that the renowned Max Born asked Oppenheimer to come and study under him at Goettingen, where in 1927 he published, in collaboration with Born, a paper on the quantum theory of molecules incorporating what would come to be known as the Born-Oppenheimer method. Oppenheimer's mentor (and now, in effect, colleague) Born, with Niels Bohr, did pioneering work on particle complementarity and the wave-particle duality of light, so that certainly Oppenheimer was in excellent company as a graduate student and developing scientist, though he sometimes felt later that he had come along just a little too late to get in on the excitement of some of the really fundamental discoveries in the field. In any case he continued his own research and received his Ph.D. in the spring of 1927, his dissertation having dealt with normalization of eigenfunctions in the theory of continuous spectra.

Though it has sometimes been said that Oppenheimer never made truly groundbreaking discoveries– unlike Thomson he didn't discover the electron, and unlike Niels Bohr and Max Born he didn't discover complementarity, and unlike these people he never won a Nobel Prize– it should be obvious to anyone with an appreciation of the science involved that the new realms he did explore were of immense importance in themselves. The building blocks of science are not always the discoveries that make headlines; often, as with Oppenheimer's work on continuous spectrum theory, the developments going on 'below the radar' journalistically are too conceptually abstruse even to get reported on. It's a little like what people used to say about Albert Einstein and the theory of relativity: everyone knows he did something but nobody quite knows what it was! (In 1939 Oppenheimer, with George Volkoff, would publish work in the area of stellar physics leading to the theory of black holes, something for which Oppenheimer is seldom given credit.)

During the period of his doctoral studies at Goettingen, Max Born and others couldn't help noticing a developing quality in Robert Oppenheimer that was destined to cause him more trouble in the years to come than he could possibly have imagined– an arrogant, strident tendency to be impatient with anyone whose comprehension of complex matters was less rapid than his own, which in practice meant that he was impatient with just about everybody. (With out-and-out stupidity of the sort he would run into in government circles, with no 'decompression period' after years of hanging around with Nobel laureates, he had no tolerance whatever, and we will see the difficulties this tendency was to lead to in the early 1950s, when, as it was to turn out, he made at least one enemy too many.)

Returning to the United States, Oppenheimer had a brief stint back at Harvard teaching some seminars and then (in 1928) moved on to the California Institute of Technology in Pasadena, where he made further discoveries regarding quantum effects relating to alpha-particle decay, and where he also started a professional love affair with the campus at Berkeley, an academic setting then so uninvolved with theoretical physics that it seemed to him to be a place to make fresh inroads. He would come to hold simultaneous professorships at Caltech and Berkeley, shuttling back and forth. But soon he was off to Europe again, this time for postdoctoral studies.

It was at Leiden in the Netherlands, studying with George Uhlenbeck, that Oppenheimer first acquired the nickname 'Oppie,' originally written 'Opje' in Dutch. The nickname would stick. (I never met the man, but as with many writers who never met him but have come to have an affinity with him nonetheless, I will take the liberty of referring to him at times by the familiar nickname.)

From Leiden he would go on to Zurich in the summer of 1929 to study with Wolfgang Pauli, a pioneer in the development of such quantum concepts as spin angular momentum. Here Oppenheimer's interest in quantum field theory really took form, and he was able to be a part of Pauli's and Heisenberg's early work on quantum electrodynamics. One has to go out of the way to remind oneself at this point that Oppie was only twenty-five years old.

When he returned to the United States it was to step back into his double academic rôle at Caltech and Berkeley, again shuttling back and forth and taking many of his students with him from one campus to the other. During the period of the early 1930s he would form some of the acquaintances, and gravitate toward some of the socio-political positions, that would give form to the rest of his life, for better or worse. It was during this time that he came to know Berkeley's Ernest Lawrence (father of the cyclotron) and Robert Serber, at that time a research assistant who came to be one of Oppenheimer's closest professional assiciates.

Not surprisingly, given such an academic setting and so impressive a circle of colleagues, the 1930s saw Oppenheimer produce a prodigious amount of research in theoretical physics, including work that foreshadowed such forthcoming developments as theories of antimatter and the quantum nature of half-spin particles, and work in nuclear physics that was edging him subtly in the direction of his later work on the atomic bomb and questions, generally, of nuclear energy. Also, as I have mentioned, his work in the late 1930s on the collapse of heavy stars led to the formulation, in cosmology theory, of the concept of 'black hole,' so called by physicist John Wheeler.

During this period, too, Oppenheimer managed to evolve from a socially uninvolved devotee of science and literature and classical languages (famously including Sanskrit) to an enthusiast of socioeconomic issues. This was in large part due to the effects of the Great Depression, which not even so insular a scholar as Oppenheimer could very well ignore forever. As with many people in those days, the conditions of life set him thinking about social and economic systems.

But it really took a young woman to make him fully aware of these things. He met Jean Tatlock in 1936, a Stanford doctoral student in her twenties and an avowed leftist– a member of the Communist Party, in fact. (This didn't mean the same thing that it would come to mean twenty years later.) They had a serious affair that never quite worked out, and Jean Tatlock, often a victim of severe depression, ultimately committed suicide (in

1941). But she had left her mark upon Oppie in terms of helping to form his political views– of which, indeed, up to that time, he had had virtually none.

It has often been forgotten that in the 1930s many people gravitated toward communist causes not out of any foreign political allegiances but out of concern with various humanitarian causes made all the more compelling by the rigors of the Depression. Such associations didn't carry the stigma, at the time, that they would have in the 1950s, when Russia had shifted from being something of a U.S. ally to being a formidable Cold War foe, and when communism had evolved from being a sort of avant-garde social movement to being a subversive and dangerous allegiance smacking of disloyalty and treason.

Oppie's own interest in the leftist world of the 1930s had a lot to do with sympathy with labor unions and with the Loyalist cause in the war in Spain, and nothing to do with political alliances hostile to the United States. This distinction, however, would be of little avail to him in the McCarthy Era witch-hunt mentality of the 1950s.

Further sealing what was to be an unfortunate political fate, Oppenheimer married a woman who had been married to a communist and had in fact been a Communist Party member herself. He met Kitty in 1939 (she had actually left the Communist Party three years before they met) and after her divorce they married, in 1940. They bought a house in Berkeley and tried to settle into a normal family life, but things didn't stay that way for long. Momentous discoveries in science and an increasingly alarming international situation were soon to change everything for them. Forever.

Suddenly (in 1939) nuclear fission had become a hot topic of discussion at Berkeley because of new experimental evidence suggesting that it might well be a reality to be reckoned with in practical terms. Characteristically, Oppie was immediately full of ideas about how this new branch of physics might work and in what directions it might go. He started off working with Ernest Lawrence at Berkeley on fission-related projects and by shortly after Pearl Harbor had assumed a leading rôle in that research under the aegis of the newly formed U.S. Office of Scientific Research and Development, which meant that the work was no longer all academic and theoretical– it had military implications, and by mid-1942 it was clear to all concerned that it was all about the feasibility of nuclear explosions and the weaponry that this notion implied.

A first-of-its-kind project was born. Its code name: Manhattan Project. Its mission: develop an atomic bomb. The person in charge was Brigadier General Leslie Groves, and the life-paths of Groves and Oppenheimer were soon to cross.

But it was really Nobel Prize winner A. H. Compton's recommendations to the National Academy of Sciences that first really brought Oppie on stage. Oppie had begun to work, essentially on his own, with Berkeley's radiation laboratory, where he made discoveries that greatly reduced the costs of separating uranium 235, and Compton was so impressed that when work clearly intended for A-bomb development really got under way, he asked Oppenheimer to work in that area full-time. In the course of these events, Oppenheimer became convinced that the efforts being exerted in this field were going to continue to be too scattered, and that if an atomic weapon was going to be developed it was going to become necessary to concentrate the work in one location. This idea quickly caught on. Compton would make the recommendation, before it even existed, that Oppie be in charge of the new facility. In the autumn of 1942 General Groves, Oppenheimer, and two military collaborators met in a reserved train compartment to begin to hammer out the first plans for establishing a group of laboratories, in some single carefully-chosen place, to give birth to the world's first atomic bomb.

    The choice of the planned facility (designated "Site Y" before it was even specified as to location) was a problem. Oak Ridge was suggested first, but for various reasons involving security, that site was rejected. After other suggestions were entertained and eliminated, Oppenheimer remembered an isolated spot, known to him from childhood, in New Mexico: the mountaintop boarding school at Los Alamos. He used to remark to friends: "My two great loves are physics and New Mexico. It's a pity they can't be combined" (Jungk, 129) and now it appeared that this rather whimsical wish might be granted after all.

    Not long after Groves' and Oppenheimer's historic train ride between Chicago and the West Coast, the two of them, together with two of the general's adjutants, made an unannounced visit to the school at Los Alamos. The site appealed to Groves right away, though mostly because at that point neither he nor anyone else fully appreciated the magnitude of the project. There were only the school buildings, thus not much of a pre-existing settlement, but Groves then thought that only a hundred or so scientists would be involved, and that these could rather easily be provided laboratories and living quarters. He had no notion that a year later 3,500 people would be there, and eventually over 6,000. (Oppie, who had no previous experience with such things, proved to be a master administrator with this group, many of whom he recruited himself.)

Wartime emergency prerogatives made it possible for the Army essentially to evict everyone from the boarding school and commandeer the spot for the construction of the needed research and development facility atop the mesa. By mid-1943, scientific work had begun at the site. There was generally a sense of some urgency about getting started, since the perception widely held was that the Nazis were already hard at work trying to develop atomic weapons in Germany.

During the winter of 1942-43, after Groves had chosen Oppenheimer to head up the atomic bomb project but before the secret installation at Los Alamos had actually opened, an incident occurred which was to haunt Oppenheimer for the rest of his life. A French professor at Berkeley, Haakon Chevalier, who had strong communist leanings, came to dinner at Robert and Kitty's home, with his wife Barbara. Sometime during the evening Chevalier told Oppenheimer that a mutual acquaintance, an engineer named George Eltenton, was interested in finding ways to convey scientific information to Russian scientists. Oppenheimer's immediate reaction was that he wanted nothing to do with such activities. Unfortunately he delayed several months in telling Army intelligence about the incident, and when he did report it he declined (at first) to name names, though eventually he did so. No real harm had been done, in terms of any sensitive information being compromised, but years later Oppenheimer would deeply regret not having told the whole story at once.

It is important to note, given the problems that were to plague Oppenheimer later, that General Groves, in placing Oppenheimer in charge of the atomic bomb project, overruled a number of his own security officers who opposed Oppie's clearance not only on rather pedestrian grounds (he was too young, he had little or no administrative experience, and he didn't have a Nobel Prize) but also because even in those days– more so with America by now formally at war– people with a lot of left-wing associations and inclinations made the security establishment nervous. Leftist political leanings had not yet acquired all the sinister 'sympathy with foreign powers' implications they would have a decade later, but they still smacked of ultra-liberal agendas that few government or military officials were comfortable with.

But, even so, Groves in effect told his more jittery fellow officers: Look, in the first place, if he can't do the job, neither can anybody else, but I think he can, and if Oppie's political views make you jumpy, you just sort all that stuff out for yourselves, because in the meantime I need this guy's brains– we've got a bomb to build. And he got his way.

Oppenheimer directed the bomb project brilliantly, coördinating all the work, maintaining morale in difficult living and working conditions, and (as physicist Hans Bette has remarked) drawing the very best out of everyone for the accomplishment of the mission, a mission brought forward under such secrecy that the people in Santa Fe just down the mountain had no idea what was being done so close by.

The morning of 16 July 1945 saw the explosion of the world's first atomic bomb at the Trinity Site in New Mexico's desertlands 300 miles south of Los Alamos. It was, as some have said, the morning the sun rose twice, and it brought to Oppenheimer's mind a line in Sanskrit from the *Bhagavad-Gita*, which he translated: "I am become death, the destroyer of worlds." (General Groves had made secret evacuation plans with the governor of New Mexico, should they be needed.)

With a dazzling flash seen even by a blind girl many miles away, officially explained as an ammunition dump having exploded, the colossal effort under Oppenheimer's inspired directorship had come to fruition, a rewarding yet chilling culmination of what had been more than two years' work in a super-secret scientific bubble where life had been in some ways surreal, with Edward Teller playing Beethoven on the piano in his shack, staff parties propelled by 200-proof lab alcohol, and all the while an urgent mission to produce 'the Gadget' before the Germans could make one, an urgency that had continued even after 7 May 1945 when the war in Europe was officially over and only the problem of Japan remained. The mushroom cloud over the desert floor was the outcome, and the world had changed forever, even though the public would still know nothing of the bomb until after Hiroshima, an experience that fate had saved not for President Franklin Roosevelt but for President Harry Truman.

With Compton, Fermi, and Lawrence, Oppenheimer served, before Hiroshima, on a Scientific Panel to the Interim Committee newly formed to advise President Truman. It was suggested that a demonstration of the new bomb might be sufficient to cause Japan to surrender, but the Panel decided otherwise— they felt that only an actual use of the weapon would end the war. Hiroshima was bombed on 6 August and Nagasaki three days later, with Japan surrendering in short order.

When Oppenheimer's rôle in the development of the weapon that had ended the war became public knowledge, which it did on the day after Hiroshima, he was a national hero of a sort never known before or since, and, for the next eight years, a continuing resource to his government as an advisor on matters of atomic weaponry and atomic energy generally, all of which should have earned him his country's undying gratitude. (Alas, in the end this was not to be the case.)

In 1946 President Truman appointed Oppenheimer to the newly formed General Advisory Committee to the (also newly formed) Atomic Energy Commission, and Oppie was quickly elected chairman of the GAC. Just two months before, the president had also named retired admiral Lewis Strauss to the AEC. If ever two people were tragically fated to have their paths cross, Oppenheimer and Strauss were so fated, with eventually disastrous results.

One at first might have thought the relationship was going to be a healthy one. Strauss in late 1946 was chairman of the search committee charged with finding a new director of the Institute for Advanced Study at Princeton, that renowned think-tank that over the years was home to Albert Einstein, Kurt Gödel, and a host of other intellectual giants. The committee unanimously authorized Strauss to offer the position to Dr. Oppenheimer, who hesitated somewhat in accepting, as he and Kitty, with their children Peter and Toni, had thought themselves pretty well settled in California. There followed some discussions, in fact, in which Oppenheimer mentioned to Strauss that the FBI had some rather derogatory files that could conceivably amount to an argument against Oppenheimer's taking the job, but Strauss replied that he had seen those files and did not consider that they had any such negative significance (Pais, 81-82). Oppenheimer became director of the Institute for Advanced Study in April of 1947. (Alas, relations with Strauss would turn very nasty a few years later.)

The penchant for administrative prowess that Oppie had exhibited at Los Alamos during the Manhattan Project years would become evident again in his directorship of the Institute at Princeton. Reminiscent of his recruiting days in New Mexico, he brought a great many impressive people to Princeton, and not all of them scientists- according to his biographer Abraham Pais, probably the first person to visit due to Oppie was the poet T.S. Eliot. In physics and mathematics, notable recruits were Freeman Dyson and computer pioneer John von Neumann, along with numerous others.

While he did not publish heavily in the professional journals during the late 1940s and early 1950s– his double duties as director of the Institute for Advanced Study and chairman of the AEC's General Advisory Committee kept him frenetically busy most of the time– Oppenheimer was delectably immersed in the world of theoretical physics, and not just as an academic abstraction but as a ponderous matter with national and international implications. He attended numerous physics conferences and still, as at Los Alamos, had the effect of urging other outstanding scientists on in the pursuit of their truths.

But the Cold War was making the world a complex and frustrating place, and for Oppenheimer in particular there were storm clouds on the horizon. As we shall see, those clouds not only threatened storms but delivered them as well.

But first a look at another realm of secrecy- one destined to be fateful for Robert Oppenheimer.

2
The Dark World of UFO Secrecy

When Pilot Kenneth Arnold, flying near Mt. Ranier on 24 June 1947, spotted nine fast-moving, crescent-shaped metallic objects in the air, and when journalist Bob Becquette coined the term 'flying saucer,' a new era of human awareness was born, at least for those open-minded enough to consider the implications– that things sometimes appear in our skies for which we cannot readily account.

A week and a half later, on the night of 4 July 1947, something anomalous crashed in the desert some distance northwest of Roswell, New Mexico, and a flurry of news surrounded the event, until General Ramey of the Eighth Air Force (acting on orders from General McMullen, who was acting on orders from Harry Truman) squelched the story on 8 July with the claim that the mysterious object was a weather balloon. Thus began a long history of official government and military cover stories that always appear, on first glance, to make everything seem ordinary; but they suffer in the end from deeply flawed internal logic, essentially because they're typically put together in haste, even in panic, with no time to script them more seamlessly. Serious UFO investigators can and do pick the bad logic apart and expose the cover stories, as in the case of Roswell, where (after over thirty years of silence on the subject) investigators have interviewed hundreds of witnesses to determine that the object in question was genuinely anomalous, that there were several diminutive bodies and acres of debris, and that the military made a concerted (if clumsy) effort to suppress the whole event.

On 25 March 1948 an unaccountable object reportedly crashed near Aztec, New Mexico. Again, there has never been an official admission that something extraordinary happened, though we have reason to believe that a great deal of government-sponsored expertise was brought to bear.

In August of 1951 at least eighteen bluish-green lights, disk-shaped objects, were seen all over west Texas flying in wing formation; numerous witnesses, many of whom I interviewed for the first time myself, gave assurance that these objects were not birds and not conventional aircraft (Burleson, 40ff). The Air Force sent investigators who ended up claiming that the 'Lubbock Lights' objects were street-lamp reflections on the bottoms of ducks. (Now *you* tell one.)

On 2 July 1952 a Navy photographer named Delbert Newhouse took moving pictures of about a dozen point-of-light objects flying crazy angular patterns near Tremonton, Utah. Officials tried to explain these objects away as seagulls, a perfectly idiotic explanation to anyone who has ever seen the Newhouse film.

On the night of 2-3 November 1957 a large oval object was seen landing at various spots on the roadways around Levelland, Texas, observed by motorists who reported experiencing what we now call the 'EM (electromagnetic) effect'– their car or truck lights dimmed, their engines spluttered or died. Sheriff Weir Clem was one of the witnesses, and was told (as his daughter Ginger told me when I interviewed her) to "drop it" or else, in precisely those terms, even though the official explanation was that what people had seen was 'ball lightning.' Again, the cover story is an insult to one's intelligence.

The pattern has continued through the years, down to the present time: reliable observers see and experience extraordinary things, and the government explains them away with cover stories that wouldn't satisfy a child. It's just too painful for them to admit that there are things happening around us over which the government has no control.

The pattern never changes. On 8 January 2008 hundreds of people saw an object possibly more than a mile wide over central Texas (reminiscent of the huge 'Phoenix Lights' object seen on 13 March 1997 in Arizona, likewise by hundreds of witnesses), and the military (as in the Phoenix case, when there were unacknowledged military alerts) out-and-out lied about it, giving out at least two mutually contradictory statements.

Any reputable UFO investigator will tell you that the vast majority of UFO sighting reports turn out to be mundanely explainable– as balloons, birds, meteors, clouds, conventional aircraft– but a select few events defy all facile attempts at explanation, and almost without exception the involvement of government in these events is characterized by deception and subterfuge.

The point, for our purposes, is that quite aside from classified weaponry and the like, the government of the United States, through events which it couldn't have expected and over which it has little or no control, has come to deal in secrecy on a scale not even imagined during the Los Alamos years, secrecy of broader implication even than nuclear weapons.

Some people have said to me: there couldn't be anything to this UFO business, because the government isn't really capable of keeping a secret. But I have the counterexample to disprove that: the Manhattan Project. If the government was capable of employing 6,000 people in Los Alamos for two years to produce an atomic bomb, when the people living right down the mountain in Santa Fe had no clue what was really going on, trust me– the government can keep a secret.

Even when– perhaps especially when– the secret is one of enormous implication, and when the necessity of keeping the secret is not a matter of the government's own choosing, but rather a consequence of things happening that could not have been anticipated. Laws have been broken, people have been threatened and even killed to keep official secrets relating to UFO events.

There is reason to believe that Robert Oppenheimer was drawn up into this web of heightened secrecy. He became its victim in a way that has never really been explored. Until now.

3.
Oppenheimer and UFO Crash Retrieval Activities

The story of how we can know about Robert Oppenheimer's involvement with UFO crash retrieval activities begins in Canada, with a man named Wilbert Smith. This matter revolves around what I call the SSS (Smith-Sarbacher-Steinman) correspondence, a remarkable and valuable interchange of letters on the subject of government involvement with unidentified flying objects.

Wilbert Smith (who died in 1962 at the age of only 52) was the Senior Radio Engineer for Canada's Department of Transport, which would later become the Department of Communications. He earned his master's degree at the University of British Columbia and was put in charge of an operation called Radio Ottawa, involving the interception of secret Soviet radio communications, so that Smith was entrusted, by the Canadian government, with highly classified information. On 21 November 1950 he wrote a top-secret memo to the Deputy Minister of Transport for Air Services, one C. P. Edwards, urging the inception of the program Project Magnet to investigate the possibility of magnetic propulsion, a principle Smith suspected was employed by UFOs. As it turned out, this program was in operation for four years with Smith as its director.

The Smith memo, had it been written and transmitted in the United States, would probably have remained classified forever, if experience with classified documents is any guide, but– the gods be praised– the Canadian government declassified it in 1978. In the process of arguing for Project Magnet, the memo mentions that while flying saucers' propulsion systems were of course unknown, they were a subject of study in the United States by "a small group headed by Doctor Vannevar Bush" (Hesemann, 81).

Of Dr. Bush we will have more to say later. The importance of the Smith memo is really that it demonstrates beyond a doubt that at least one national government, that of Canada, took the technical study of UFOs seriously and in fact actively engaged in it.

But even prior to composing the memo, Wilbert Smith had also wanted to try to get in touch with scientists who had actually investigated crashed UFOs, and for this purpose he went through some contacts at the Canadian Embassy in Washington to obtain an appointment with Dr. Robert Sarbacher, who was scientific advisor to the Research and Development Commission in the U.S. Department of Defense. Sarbacher, who was a professor at Harvard and maintained an office at the Pentagon, was a highly respected scientist. Smith met with him on 15 September 1950 and kept detailed notes on their conversation.

After some preliminary exchanges of remarks

about the existence of flying saucers, Smith said to Sarbacher: "I understand the whole subject of saucers is classified." Significantly for the observations I will make later with regard to Oppenheimer's situation, Sarbacher replied: "Yes, it is classified two points higher even than the H-bomb. In fact it is the most highly classified subject in the U.S. Government at the present time" (Hesemann, 80-81). Sarbacher was then unwilling to provide any more information, but Smith mostly had what he had come for, and when he wrote his now famous memo to his own government, he used Sarbacher's remarks as a selling point, and evidently they had the desired effect, since the government of Canada did put Project Magnet into effect.

In 1978, through a well-known UFO investigator, the late Leonard Stringfield, the declassified Smith memo together with Smith's detailed notes on his conversation with Dr. Sarbacher came to the attention of a writer named William Steinman, who himself wrote to Sarbacher looking for more information about the "small group" of researchers to which Smith had alluded in his memo.

On 29 October 1983 Sarbacher, writing on a letter-head reading "Washington Institute of Technology, Oceanography, and Physical Sciences," replied, telling Steinman that in the late 1940s and early 1950s a good many prominent scientists were involved in one way or another with the study of crashed disks. He further said that meetings occurred among these scientists, at Wright Field (later called Wright-Patterson Air Force Base) in Ohio, and although Sarbacher had not (he said) attended these meetings himself, other notable names were involved: "I can only say this: John von Neumann and Dr. Vannevar Bush were definitely involved, and I think Dr. Robert Oppenheimer also" (Hesemann, 83-84).

I should mention here that Oppenheimer's being present at such meetings would only in part have been possible due to his high-level security clearance; the other half of the formula– always, with classified information– is *need to know*. And clearly if military officials at Wright Field were convinced that Oppenheimer, a civilian scientist, had the need to know crash retrieval information, it could scarcely have been for any other reason than his being involved, or about to become involved, in those retrieval activities themselves.

One can well imagine President Truman's getting a phone call in the wee hours of 4-5 July 1947: "Mr. President, we have a problem. Something has crashed in the desert in New Mexico, and we think it's not from anywhere on this planet." What would he do? He would call in experts. Whom would he call? People most highly qualified to study the problem *and* already cleared. Close to the top of that list one would certainly have found the name J. Robert Oppenheimer, so that Sarbacher's mention of Oppenheimer is very much in keeping with any feasible scenario we may associate with the whole situation of crashed UFOs in the late 1940s.

Another Oppenheimer connection of sorts

turned up in February 1990 when UFO researcher Kevin Randle interviewed a man named Steve Lytle, the son of a mathematician who at one time had worked with Oppie. Lytle told Randle that his father had shown him a piece of Roswell UFO debris bearing inscriptions that the mathematician had been asked to decipher, without success as it turned out (Randle and Schmitt, 65). One wonders whether Oppenheimer knew of this project through his association with Lytle, especially given what we find described in William Steinman's book.

Steinman, the writer who saw the Wilbert Smith memo and communicated with Dr. Sarbacher to hear that Oppenheimer and others were involved in crash retrieval activities, was particularly interested in the Aztec, New Mexico UFO crash of March 1948, and wrote a book called *UFO Crash at Aztec* with, significantly, a foreword written by well-known UFO investigator Leonard H. Stringfield, a specialist himself on crash retrievals (and author of a 1977 book about UFOs, called *Situation Red*).

Len Stringfield was a field investigator for NICAP (the National Investigations Committee on Aerial Phenomena) for many years, having previously worked with the Air Force in an off-the-record case-reporting capacity and thus having gained experience with a vast number of UFO sighting cases. He was strictly a no-nonsense guy, meticulous in his analysis and his methods, and careful unfailingly to separate the fanciful from the factual, the well-attested case from the hoax, the crackpot wannabee 'witness' from the reliable observer.

So, in my estimation, Stringfield's remarks in the foreword to Steinman's book are deserving of serious attention. For one thing, Stringfield (going against the pattern of foreword writers generally) is *critical* of Steinman in a way- not critical of the contents of the book, but critical of the fact that Steinman might have written about the Aztec crash retrieval in a manner more conducive to being believed: "[U]nfortunately, some of his key informants remain anonymous. A few he has revealed to me in confidence by letter; others, no, being too sensitive he claims" (Steinman, 21). Further: "[O]f greater concern is Steinman's narrative style used in his early chapters- assumptive and matter-of-fact- where he covers the sensitive issues. . . . I may know some of his unnamed sources, but the reader, who doesn't, may not only question the narrative style but the book's credibility as well. Steinman would have been wiser, I believe, had he made even the vaguest references to a source; something, perhaps, like this: '. . . according to the younger sister, living in Paducah, of the ex-wife of my source, Dr. F.O.O., who now lives with her older sister in Peoria.' That one, Bill, would have thrown everyone off and still, in all honesty, be accurate, and it might just have appeased the reader" (Steinman, 22).

We UFO investigators have all experienced the problem of important witnesses who quite understandably don't want to be identified, and Len Stringfield was right to express it as a concern with regard to Steinman's unidentified sources- who had, however, some of them, been identified to

-28-

Stringfield. My point is that Stringfield, an experienced and reliable investigator with high standards of truthfulness, was confident enough of the veracity of Steinman's claims to lend his own name to them by way of the foreword, and to be upfront about his own concerns over Steinman's practice– unfortunately probably necessary, due to issues of confidentiality– of not sharing sources with his readers. (Every serious UFO investigator soon learns that many witnesses absolutely refuse to have their names more widely known, and no UFO investigator worthy of the name ever identifies a witness who wishes not to be identified.)

So let us see what Steinman tells us.

On 25 March 1948 three separate radar units tracked an unidentified flying object in the Four Corners area of northwestern New Mexico; triangulation revealed that the object had apparently come down near the town of Aztec. A message went out to the Secretary of State, General George Marshall, who contacted Truman's special advisory group MJ-12 and also alerted the special Army counterintelligence group known as IPU, the Interplanetary Phenomenon Unit, instituted shortly after the Roswell incident. As science-fiction-ish as the name of this unit sounds, its existence was confirmed on 25 September 1980 by the Army director of counterintelligence in reply to a FOIA (Freedom of Information Act) request by veteran UFO researcher Richard Hall (Wood, 4). In 1948 the IPU's home base was Camp Hale, Colorado, which I have found to have been at one time (several years later than the Aztec incident) a CIA training base well chosen for its geographical remoteness and rugged terrain.

The authorities at Camp Hale dispatched a military scout team by helicopter to the crash site some twelve miles northeast of Aztec, New Mexico. This team reported spotting the object, a domed disk about 100 feet in diameter, whereupon General Marshall cut off all communications except between IPU and himself, and issued a 'false alarm' cover story to the radar stations that had tracked the object. A commando-style recovery team then headed out from Camp Hale, and meanwhile Dr. Vannevar Bush, head of the government's Joint Research and Development Board, was directed to put together a second team, this one purely scientific, to send to the crash site. Bush immediately assembled the team, which he headed up himself: mathematician and computer designer Dr. John von Neumann, biophysicist Dr. Detlev Bronk, geophysicist Dr. Lloyd Berkner, geophysicist Dr. Carl Hieland, inorganic chemist Dr. Horace Buele van Volkenburgh, aeronautical engineer Dr. Jerome Hunsaker, and– along with a few other specialists– Dr. J. Robert Oppenheimer. All were of course immediately sworn to the utmost secrecy (Steinman, 27ff).

The scientists were assembled at the airfield on the outskirts of Durango, Colorado, some thirty-five miles, by unimproved dirt roads, north of the site. Shortly after the military recovery team arrived and sealed off the area (bringing in trucks disguised as oil drilling equipment), Bush's scientific team arrived too and began their work. They found at least fourteen charred, diminutive bodies (which Dr. Bronk would examine), along with instrument panels bearing hieroglyphic-style symbols that Oppenheimer thought somewhat to resemble Sanskrit, a language with which he was familiar. A sort of book with plastic-like pages also turned up with the same sort of Sanskrit-like symbols. (This was eventually turned over to prominent cryptanalysts William Friedman and Lambros Callihamos for decipherment, but if they made any progress, the results are classified.) After three days of preliminary analysis, the craft and the bodies were stealthily moved to Los Alamos for storage and further study.

Thus if Steinman's unnamed sources were authentic– and, again, Len Stringfield's involvement lends a great deal of extra credibility to the proposition– we are left with the awareness that Oppenheimer was intimately involved in the Aztec, New Mexico UFO crash retrieval as well as the Roswell retrieval.

I will add that Stringfield not only knew and respected many of Steinman's sources, but also did his own research work on the case. He interviewed a retired University of South Florida professor named Robert Spencer Carr, who claimed to know five participants in the UFO recovery activity of 1948. Stringfield implored Dr. Carr to identify his primary source, and when Carr did so, Stringfield was "dumbfounded. I knew his name well in research, and recalled some of his comments on UFOs while he served as an Air Force officer." Carr, however, asked Stringfield not to use the name of the source, who he said "participated in the 1948 retrieval and saw alien bodies on location" (Good, 393). Two of Carr's sources were aeronautical engineers and another– the one who *was* identified– was Arthur Bray, a security guard involved in the Aztec recovery.

Another Carr (secondary) witness was the daughter of a man present at the recovery; the woman's father had once remarked to her that it would destroy the oil industry if the Aztec craft's propulsion system had become common knowledge in the scientific community. It seems reasonable to me that this alone would have been sufficient for the whole matter to have been kept top secret, and indeed I will argue that this 'propulsion physics wrinkle' may well have been the decisive element that got Oppenheimer in so much difficulty later on. (Oppenheimer, examining the Aztec object's propulsion system, would have understood its stupendous economic implications right away.)

Between them, Steinman and Stringfield found a number of witnesses who know the location of the crash site in Hart Canyon near Aztec, including at least one observer who saw the object in flight. One gathers that the Aztec event is well supported by witness testimony, and was an event in which Oppenheimer found himself weirdly enmeshed, no doubt to his fascination as a scientist. He would in time pay a heavy price, however, for his participation in the Roswell retrieval and in Vannevar Bush's Aztec scientific recovery team, or so I would argue from an examination of the facts. It is possible for a scientist, in the ardor of his professional interests, not to recognize when he is beginning to enter realms that are unhealthy to enter, in terms of the strange world of government secrecy, and such, I believe, was Oppie's situation.

Certain members of that Vannevar Bush team– in particular Bronk, Berkner, Hunsaker, and Bush himself– were, significantly, also members of a larger 'inside group' that would come to have great significance for Oppie in his hour of distress six years down the road. For our purposes, it will be important to understand who and what this group was.

4.
MJ-12: Truman's Insiders

Imagine yourself as President Harry Truman on the night of the Roswell UFO crash in July 1947. Sometime after midnight you get a phone call that will change your life and your view of the world forever, and you have only minutes to decide what, immediately, you should do. To get things rolling on that night, at least, you send orders down the chain of command to have a military recovery operation under way, picking up the pieces, and you arrange for an elite group of scientists to go in and examine the debris and the bodies. These people must possess the requisite knowledge, and they must already have high security clearances. As you go into a huddle with your advisors about whom to choose, the name Robert Oppenheimer comes readily to mind, among others.

But during the days that follow, you realize that more is required– this is not going to be a short-term problem only, and you must assemble a group of carefully chosen people, both military and civilian, to oversee, and to advise you on, matters relating to extraterrestrial spacecraft retrieval and analysis. You make your choice: twelve 'insiders' who have a mission never before imparted to any group by any president.

So far this may sound like abstract speculation, but in December 1984 it became more than that, when film director Jaime Shandera received, in the mail, a roll of undeveloped black-and-white 35 mm film in a plain brown envelope bearing an Albuquerque postmark but no return address. When developed, the film turned out to contain eight pages of government documents marked TOP SECRET / MAJIC, in the manner of special-access classifications frequently used in restricted materials, where a code word (like the now well-known but once carefully guarded UMBRA or ULTRA; in this case MAJIC) is used to specify that only a certain narrowly defined *and* properly cleared group of people have the need to know the contents of the documents, i.e. in contrast with the notion that just anybody with a certain level of clearance might have access to them. (This is a practice very familiar to me, as I was in an Air Force intelligence unit in the 1960s and have seen such classification-level-with-codeword stamps on innumerable Secret and Top Secret documents.)

The documents in the Shandera package, when made more widely known, engendered a great deal of excitement. While some people in the field of UFO studies have, in the spirit of healthy and constructive skepticism, questioned the validity of the MAJIC documents, a number of researchers– notably Stanton Friedman, Dr. Robert Wood and Ryan Wood– have invested a great deal of time and labor in determining that the documents are genuine. Stan Friedman in particular, working with the styles and type fonts and general formatting of the documents and placing them in historical and usage-based perspective by comparisons with other documents, has argued tirelessly for the authenticity of the MAJIC documents, and I am strongly inclined– with no disrespect intended toward researchers who feel otherwise– to agree with Friedman's assessments. One may read a detailed account of Friedman's authentication of these documents in his book *Flying Saucers and Science* (pp. 257-95).

The title page to the document package bears the words
BRIEFING DOCUMENT: OPERATION MAJESTIC 12
PREPARED FOR PRESIDENT-ELECT DWIGHT D. EISENHOWER: (EYES ONLY)
18 NOVEMBER, 1952

The page following bears the subject line OPERATION MAJESTIC-12 PRELIMINARY BRIEFING FOR PRESIDENT-ELECT EISENHOWER and identifies the briefing officer as ADM. ROSCOE H. HILLENKOETTER (MJ-1). The text reads:

OPERATION MAJESTIC-12 is a TOP SECRET research and Development / Intelligence operation responsible directly and only to the President of the United States. Operations of the project are carried out under control of the Majestic-12 (Majic-12) Group which was established by special classified executive order of President Truman on 24 September, 1947, upon recommendation by Dr. Vannevar Bush and Secretary James Forrestal. . . . Members of the Majestic-12 Group were designated as follows:

Adm. Roscoe H. Hillenkoetter
Dr. Vannevar Bush
Secy. James V. Forrestal
Gen. Nathan F. Twining
Gen. Hoyt S. Vandenberg
Dr. Detlev Bronk
Dr. Jerome Hunsaker
Mr. Sidney W. Souers
Mr. Gordon Gray
Dr. Donald Menzel
Gen. Robert M. Montague
Dr. Lloyd V. Berkner

The death of Secretary Forrestal on 22 May, 1949, created a vacancy which remained unfilled until 01 August, 1950, upon which date Gen. Walter B. Smith was designated as permanent replacement (Friedman, 222-23).

    Note that four of these people– Bush, Bronk, Hunsaker, and Berkner– were named, in William Steinman's account, as being members (along with Robert Oppenheimer) of the scientific team sent to the Aztec impact site. Another name on the list– Gordon Gray– assumes great significance later, in terms of what would happen to Oppenheimer.
    Briefly, let's see who these people were.
    Admiral Roscoe Hillenkoetter (MJ-1) was an Annapolis graduate and the first director of the Central Intelligence Agency (CIA) when it replaced the Central Intelligence Group in 1947. He later served on the board of directors of NICAP, the National Investigations Committee for Aerial Phenomena, headed by Donald Keyhoe.

Dr. Vannevar Bush (MJ-2), was at one time dean of MIT and, along with John von Neumann, an early developer of computers. He had been the chairman of the National Advisory Committee on Aeronautics (NACA), the wartime director of the Office of Scientific Research and Development (and chairman of the organization it evolved into after World War II, the Joint Research and Development Board, out of which grew the Atomic Energy Commission). Remember, Dr. Bush was also named as the head of the "small group" mentioned in the Wilbert Smith memo as studying UFO propulsion systems.

James Forrestal (MJ-3) was appointed Undersecretary of the Navy by President Franklin Roosevelt and became full Secretary of the Navy in 1944. President Truman appointed him as the country's first Secretary of Defense. Apparently suffering from a nervous breakdown, he was hospitalized in March 1949 and (presumably) committed suicide two months later in a fall from a hospital window under circumstances so strange that many (myself included) have suspected he was murdered. He was reportedly keeping a diary at the time of his death, and it has never turned up.

General Nathan Twining (MJ-4) had a distinguished military career. He served as head of the Air Materiel Command, as Air Force Chief of Staff, and as head of the Joint Chiefs of Staff. It is highly probable that he went to New Mexico to check out the crash retrieval at Roswell (Friedman, 42). Twining had served on the National Advisory Committee on Aeronautics.

As had General Hoyt Vandenberg (MJ-5), a West Point graduate who had served as Director of Central Intelligence and as Air Force Chief of Staff; upon his death General Twining would succeed him as Chief of Staff.

Dr. Detlev Bronk (MJ-6), who would later be president of the National Academy of Sciences, served as an advisor to three presidents (starting with Truman), was president of Johns Hopkins University and of Rockefeller University; and like some of the other Majestic-12 members, he served on the NACA. Appropriately enough in terms of the possible need to study alien bodies in UFO crash retrieval operations, his specialty was aviation physiology. In fact, according to William Steinman's sources, Dr. Bronk examined the bodies at the Aztec crash site (Steinman, 39-40).

Dr. Jerome Hunsaker (MJ-7) was head of aerodynamics at MIT, succeeded Vannevar Bush as head of NACA, and was deeply involved in aircraft design. Hunsaker was the last of the Majestic-12 people to die, and it may or may not be coincidental (one suspects it wasn't) that it was shortly after Hunsaker's death in 1984 that Jaime Shandera received the film with the MJ-12 documents.

Sidney Souers (MJ-8) was a retired Navy admiral whom Truman appointed as the first director of the Central Intelligence Group (the forerunner of the CIA) and later as the first director of the National Security Council. He would maintain advisory capacities to both Truman and Eisenhower.

Gordon Gray (MJ-9) was in some ways one of

the most low-profile yet most influential of the Majestic group, active throughout his career in intelligence matters. He chaired the committee that ran covert operations for the NSC and CIA and personally managed exceedingly sensitive intelligence problems. He would become Secretary of the Army and head of the Psychological Strategy Board of the CIA, among many other positions. And in Oppenheimer's life, he would become the most important of the MJ-12 people, as we shall see.

Dr. Donald Menzel (MJ-10), however, was in a sense the most *bizarre* inclusion on the MJ-12 list. For my money, he was the original two-faced disinformation artist *par excellence*, a standard for all future such people to look up to. Or down to. Menzel was a professor of astronomy at Harvard and, in the public eye, an outspoken UFO skeptic and debunker, authoring several books purporting to trash the whole notion of flying saucers. When *not* in the public eye he did extensive highly classified consulting work for the CIA and the NSA (National Security Agency) and functioned as an expert in the science of cryptography. Menzel, in writings that debunk UFOs, employs various kinds of impressive-sounding pseudo-science widely refuted by such other science writers as Bruce Maccabee, yet widely accepted by the less scientifically knowledgeable public. Thus Menzel publicly disparaged the field of UFO studies while participating in it at the highest levels as a member of MJ-12. In short, he was a high-priced professional hypocrite. One gathers that such people have since become commonplace in government.

General Robert Montague (MJ-11) was the commander of the Ft. Bliss army base at El Paso, was responsible for the White Sands Proving Ground, and was head of the Armed Forces Special Weapons Center at Sandia Base (near Albuquerque, New Mexico), the forerunner of Sandia National Laboratory. Montague was an accomplished mathematician and was knowledgeable on the subject of nuclear weapons.

Dr. Lloyd Berkner (MJ-12) was a pilot, polar expeditions participant, and a scientist who in 1958 would head up the Interrnational Geophysical Year program for the U.S. Over the years he served on many government advisory committees, including the Robertson Panel (1953), which was convened purportedly to study the UFO question but in fact was essentially a sham.

So these were the people whom Truman appointed to his special cadre of insiders to deal with UFO-related problems. As we have noted, Robert Oppenheimer was acquainted with several of the scientists on the list, and as we shall see, some of the others– in particular Gordon Gray– would come to play important rôles in Oppie's life in the security clearance matter of 1954.

One other person, someone not a member of MJ-12, should be mentioned here: Robert Cutler, who later would write a book titled *No Time for Rest* about his extensive experience in government.

Cutler was an ex-general who worked in government service after World War II and became

President Eisenhower's Special Assistant for National Security, having served as a liaison between the National Security Council and the president. In the field of UFO studies, Cutler is well known for a memorandum that he is known to have sent to General Nathan Twining on 14 July 1954. The subject line of the Cutler-Twining Memo (there are actually two such memos, but this is the one with which we more need to concern ourselves) reads: "NSC / MJ-12 Special Studies Project," and the body of the memo itself reads:

The President has decided that the MJ-12 SSP briefing should take place *during* the already scheduled White House meeting of July 16, rather than following it as previously intended. More precise arrangements will be explained to you upon arrival. Please alter your plans accordingly.

Your concurrence in the above change of arrangements is assumed.
    ROBERT CUTLER
    Special Assistant to the President

The significance of this Top Secret memo is of course that it acknowledges the workaday reality of the group MJ-12. Cutler himself will have a special significance in the Oppenheimer affair, as we shall observe later.

I will mention a curious historical footnote with regard to Robert Cutler: that his name ends up being used, apparently as a sort of mysterious in-joke, in the classic 1951 science-fiction film *The Day the Earth Stood Still*, probably the definitive flying saucer movie of the era. In this film, the officer (played by an actor named Freeman Lusk) in charge of the problems posed by the arrival of 'spaceman' Klaatu, is one General Cutler. His name does not appear in the original screenplay (of which I have a copy), so it was apparently added later in the shooting script, for whatever reasons. It has been rumored for years that the CIA partly funded this film as a public-awareness attitude-acclimatization effort, and once when I submitted a FOIA request to the CIA asking whether this was the case, I received a 'we can neither confirm nor deny'-type response. Most UFO searchers, myself included, consider such responses to mean a sort of undocumentable 'yes,' part of what seems to me to be the strange three-valued logic that one sees employed by secretive government agencies, where the possibilities are 'true,' 'false,' and the 'undocumentably true' option I mentioned, which seems to mean something like: "The answer to your question [wink, wink] might well be yes, but if you say we said yes, we'll say we didn't exactly say that."

In any case it is clear that by the late 1940s and early 1950s the whole world of government secrecy was taking some very peculiar turns.

5
Eisenhower Drops his own Bomb

When Dr. Robert Oppenheimer was appointed director of the Los Alamos atomic bomb project in 1942, some military officials were already a bit nervous about his left-wing enthusiasms and his communist relatives and friends, but his boss General Leslie Groves overruled their objections, telling one and all that whatever Oppenheimer's problematic socio-political philosophy might be, the government of the United States badly needed his unique expertise and talents. History of course shows that this judgment call was right on the money; Oppie pushed the development of the atomic bomb through to fruition and, at the consequent victory over Japan and conclusion of World War II, became a national hero.

During the post-war years he continued to serve his government– they continually sought and received his advice and consultation on matters relating to nuclear energy, and, as has been noted, Truman appointed him to the Atomic Energy Commission's General Advisory Committee. Because of his access to sensitive information and the dubiousness of some of his past relationships and acquaintances, however, the FBI kept wiretap surveillance on him for years but never found any reason to question his loyalty or discretion. In 1947 his security status was routinely re-examined and he was approved for the Q-clearance needed for top-secret work with nuclear data.

Behind the scenes, though, trouble was brewing. Serious trouble.

Oppenheimer had enemies, and the fact that his term on the AEC's General Advisory Committee (GAC) was to expire in the summer of 1952 gave his detractors a shot at him. Edward Teller, in particular, had never forgiven Oppie for not appointing him to head up the theoretical division at Los Alamos, naming the arguably better qualified Hans Bethe instead. (No doubt it soured Teller even more to remember that at Los Alamos, Bethe had had to ask him to leave the theoretical division because he, Teller, insisted on trying to push his pet idea, the thermonuclear bomb, rather than helping with the immediate work of the team.) Teller at some point began stealthily putting the word around in high places (including the FBI) that Oppenheimer should not be reappointed to the GAC, making the preposterous argument that Oppenheimer's well-known reservations about development of the H-bomb had been movivated by "personal vanity"– by a desire not to have his own Los-Alamos-developed atomic bomb 'trumped' by a more powerful weapon (McMillan, 146).

This charge was an outrageously demeaning one– the sort of thing one would expect a not terribly bright child to hurl at a classmate on the playground– especially when one considers that, at least prior to a presidential order to go ahead with a crash H-bomb program, the *entire* GAC had opposed the development of the H-bomb on the basis that it would interfere with the development of the smaller tactical nuclear weapons that the military needed. Apparently only Oppenheimer and a few other people, having a scientific understanding of just how colossally powerful such a weapon would be, were in a position to understand that the H-bomb could never be a tactical weapon. You don't drop an H-bomb on a machine gun nest or on a bridge– you drop it on a country, or on a continent. Its only possible use is genocide; if genocide is what one wants to do, it's the perfect weapon.

But however ridiculous Teller's accusations were, they were also effective, unfortunately. Teller was intensely, I would say even pathologically, jealous of Oppenheimer's position in the scientific community and in the public eye, and sadly was determined to upstage him. The ripple effect of Teller's criticisms soon involved a number of influential people, including National Security Adviser Sidney Souers (a member of MJ-12, as we have seen), who advised the president not to reappoint Oppenheimer. In short order, Oppie was off the AEC's General Advisory Committee.

There was more trouble to come. William Liscum Borden, who served as executive director of the Joint Committee on Atomic Energy in Congress, had for some time been brooding over Oppenheimer's fitness for government service in sensitive areas of concern, and Teller egged him on in these doubts, essentially of course for purposes of Teller's own self-promotion. The AEC's Lewis Strauss and others wanted to 'groom' Teller to replace Oppenheimer as the popular American scientist icon. Bordon also conferred with AEC chairman Strauss, whom Oppenheimer had deeply and permanently alienated by mocking and humiliating him in front of a Congressional committee (Oppie could bring a lot of grief upon himself at times with these displays of scorn), and Strauss of course further deepened Borden's doubts about Oppenheimer.

Borden, in fact, became a key player when on 7 November 1953 he wrote a letter to the Federal Bureau of Investigation accusing Oppenheimer of being "more probably that not . . . an agent of the Soviet Union." This was unsupported by any evidence and in fact was wholly untrue, but that didn't seem to bother Mr. Borden, who also said, in the same letter, that "Oppenheimer has not made major contributions to the advancement of science." (Borden, a lawyer and a non-scientist, showed incredible presumption in undertaking to judge Oppenheimer in this way– as charitably as I can put it, this guy wouldn't have known real science at Oppenheimer's level of sophistication if it walked up and bit him on the butt.) Borden further said that he based his suspicions on various factors, e.g. that Oppenheimer "had no close friends except Communists" (an outright lie) and "was in frequent contact with Soviet espionage agents" (another lie) and "worked tirelessly, from January 31, 1950 onward, to retard the United States H-bomb program" (another lie) and was (another) a "hardened Communist" (Polenberg, 304-06) who had probably passed espionage information along to the Russians, an accusation that, had it been true, would have opened Robert Oppenheimer up to charges of treason punishable by a long prison sentence, or even death. However, even the inquisitional panel that would soon pontificate over Oppenheimer's career would decline to take the more rabid accusations of this delusional zealot seriously.

Nevertheless, idiotic as it was, Borden's letter in the short run had the desired effect of starting in earnest to derail Oppenheimer's life. J. Edgar Hoover at the FBI sent the letter on to the president and the Atomic Energy Commission, and things were on their way to hell-in-a-basket for Oppie. In an age of wide-eyed commie-scare McCarthy paranoia, Borden's libelous letter was like dropping a match onto dry kindling.

Another complication arose, in the person of Lewis Strauss. President Eisenhower offered the chairmanship of the Atomic Energy Commission to Strauss, but Strauss had a condition: he would not accept so long as Oppenheimer still had any rôle to play at all in the U.S. nuclear weapons program (McMillan, 170). Clearly, Strauss had never forgiven Oppenheimer for humiliating him in front of a Congressional committee. Little by little, all these influences were chipping away at Oppenheimer's reputation and career prospects, and the culmination was a White House meeting on 3 December 1953 to which Lewis Strauss was summoned.

When he arrived, he found himself in a huddle with President Eisenhower, Attorney General Herbert Brownell, Secretary of Defense Charles Wilson, and– significantly, I will argue– special security adviser Robert Cutler, the author of the Cutler-Twining Memo referencing the UFO-related group Majestic 12. The topic of discussion was J. Robert Oppenheimer, and in the course of that meeting Eisenhower made the decision to suspend Oppenheimer's security clearance, ordering the lowering of a "blank wall" between Oppenheimer and *all* government secrets (Jungk, 317-18).

It's a little hard to imagine this whole thing happening quite the same way if Truman had remained president after 1952. When Eisenhower came in, as an ex-military leader still having many close personal ties to the military, he was bound to have different views of UFO secrecy, which, I am arguing, is what a good deal of this business was really about.

In December of 1953 Eisenhower and his close advisors wanted to find a way to rescind the clearance permanently without attracting a lot of public attention, which they feared would involve adverse publicity– not an unfounded fear, obviously, considering the underhanded treatment Oppie was receiving at their hands. Opinions varied, with Robert Cutler thinking that the best approach would be to meet quietly with Oppie, explain to him that his clearance was being permanently revoked, and try to convince him not to exercise his right to fight the decision. Cutler knew that, all things considered, a lot of publicity over this could be dangerous.

The whole thing stank of subterfuge and below-the-belt collusion. Lewis Strauss, who had suggested the 'blank wall' directive to begin with in a prior meeting on 2 December, lied about the matter in his 1963 book *Men and Decisions*, covering up his 2 December meeting with the president, suggesting that he had only been present at the 3 December meeting, and trying his best to leave the impression that he not only had nothing to do with the decision to suspend Oppenheimer's clearance but was extremely upset about it (McMillan, 178-81). To put it as gently as I know how, he acted like a total jerk.

Having been traveling abroad, Oppenheimer himself was not told about the suspension of his clearance until 21 December 1953, when Strauss summoned him to a meeting at which AEC general manager Kenneth Nichols was also present. They presented Oppenheimer with the draft of a letter by Nichols outlining the charges against him, "raising questions as to your veracity, conduct and even your loyalty" (Jungk, 319). It would be funny to point out, if it were not so pitiable, that one of the reasons given, in Nichols' letter, for (in effect) planning to kick Oppenheimer out of government service was this: "It was reported that you were a subscriber to the *Daily People's World*, a west coast Communist newspaper, in 1941 and 1942" (Polenberg, 6). (In America a man can have his professional career essentially ended because he once subscribed to a *newspaper*? Give me a break. But such was the paranoid hysteria of the times. One hears accounts, from the McCarthy era, of a woman who lost her job because she had books written by certain authors on her bookshelf, or a man who lost his security clearance because he was an atheist. It was not an age in which sanity or clarity of vision necessarily prevailed.)

Strauss and Nichols gave him one day to decide whether to resign (as a consultant to the AEC) of his own accord or submit to hearings with a loyalty board to adjudicate the matter.

Oppenheimer replied the next day with a letter to Strauss in which he said, with regard to the suggestion that he make matters simple and just resign instead of putting up a fight:

> I have thought most earnestly of the alternative suggested. Under the circumstances this course of action would mean that I accept and concur in the view that I am not fit to serve the government, that I have now served for some twelve years. This I cannot do. (Jungk, 319)

To his great credit, Oppie was not in the least inclined to just roll over and die for them. There was going to be a fight.

Whether he was right in insisting on waging this battle, or whether he might have been better advised just to describe the bunch of them, to the press, as blithering idiots, is something that could be debated forever in terms of outcomes. Certainly the outcome following from the decision Oppie did make was not a happy one. But one suspects that just to acquiesce in their diminution of him as a citizen would have been worse.

In any case, battle lines were being drawn.

6
The AEC Hearing: A Travesty in Several Acts

After Oppenheimer had decided to undergo a hearing with the Atomic Energy Commission's Personnel Security Board to try to get the suspension of his clearance reversed, a date of 12 April 1954 was set for the hearing. These proceedings (as the board itself continually reminded everyone) were not supposed to be a trial, but rather an inquiry to establish the truth about Oppenheimer's fitness to continue to be privy to highly sensitive government information. The proceedings, however, which would run for three and a half weeks from 12 April to 6 May, turned out to be a trial– but in some respects the sort of trial one might expect to see in some dismal banana republic rather than in the United States of America.

Oppenheimer's own legal team (in effect, attorneys for the defense) would be headed by Lloyd Garrison, assisted by Herbert Marks, Samuel Silverman, and Allan Ecker. The attorney heading up the team retained by the AEC to represent their own side of the hearing (wicked tongues might call him the prosecuting attorney) was Roger Robb, to be assisted by Carl Arthur Rolander, Jr. There was also to be a classification officer who on occasion during the proceedings would declassify certain documents on the spot, which meant that the AEC's attorneys (who were cleared) often had prior acquaintance with documents to which Oppenheimer's attorneys (who were *not* cleared) did not have prior acquaintance.

The Personnel Security Board itself, presiding over the hearing (and analogous to the rôle of judge in a trial) consisted of a chairman seated in the middle, flanked by the other members: Ward Evans and Thomas Morgan. And the chairman himself?

Gordon Gray.

When I first read that a man named Gordon Gray had presided over Oppie's hearing, my first thought was: Nah, couldn't be the same guy. It couldn't be the Gordon Gray who was a member of Majestic 12.

But it was.

It is critically important, for our purposes here, to keep firmly in mind, when considering the details of the AEC hearing, that the presiding officer Gordon Gray *would have known everything about any involvement Oppenheimer had had in UFO crash retrievals.* There is, in my estimation, an excellent chance that this fact was of high significance in terms of the way things turned out for Oppenheimer. In describing the progress of the AEC hearing, I will sometimes choose passages that seem particularly significant with the Majestic-12 backdrop and Oppie's crash retrieval experiences in mind.

It must be understood that the transcripts of the AEC-Oppenheimer hearing were voluminous, and they have, at this writing, never been completely declassified and may well never be. (When I submitted a FOIA request that the rest of the

-53-

transcripts be declassified and released, nothing was forthcoming.) Even the parts available are massive. The original 15 June 1954 Government Printing Office version ran to 992 pages, likewise the MIT Press reprint in 1970, both of which were quickly out of print. The Richard Polenberg edition of 2002 is a judicious selection running to 352 pages (plus post-hearing correspondence) and has the attraction of brief biographical sketches of the witnesses. In all these editions, omitted classified portions (in some cases entire pages) are indicated by strings of asterisks [* * *].

The *complete* transcripts, including the classified parts withheld from publication, were more voluminous still, of course. The Gordon Gray papers reside in a special collection at the Dwight D. Eisenhower Library at Abilene, Kansas. When I checked with this library I discovered that Gordon Gray, as a condition of his contributing his papers, had stipulated that the Oppenheimer hearing transcripts be *permanently withheld from research use*. The library's own description of the pertinent documents specifies that in the Gray papers, Series IV ("The J. Robert Oppenheimer Case 1954-75") has a Subseries B that "consists of the PSB hearing transcripts and has been withdrawn in its entirety. These transcripts contain unpublished portions which may relate to national security." The library catalog lists, for the withdrawn Subseries B, nineteen volumes of "Oppenheimer Hearing Transcript" documents running to 3,314 pages.

Obvious a *lot* of material remains classified. One may well wonder *why*.

In any event, it is my wish here, with regard to what we *do* know about the hearing (which is a great deal), to provide a fair representation in only a few pages, of what happened.

During the four months preceding the opening of the hearing, Oppenheimer made various preparations. From the beginning, the FBI had him under electronic surveillance, following every detail of his search for an attorney and, after he had secured legal representation, even listening in on his defense preparations with Garrison and his associates. J. Edgar Hoover had his AEC-liaison agent Charles Bates constantly delivering surveillance reports and other FBI communiqués to AEC attorney Roger Robb, so that the prosecution (one may as well call it that) knew everything in advance about the planned defense, while the defense side worked in the dark.

It goes without saying that all of this was flagrantly illegal, and that the bunch of them– including J. Edgar Hoover himself– should have been made to answer serious criminal charges. The tactics of these people were so shabby that two decades later Roger Robb, by now United States Court of Appeals judge for the District of Columbia, when asked if he would be interested in the possibility of an appointment to the Supreme Court, turned it down– almost certainly because in the scrutiny of his record that this would have entailed, his 1954 use of illegally obtained evidence against Oppenheimer would inevitably have come out (McMillan, 200).

But in 1954 these weasels got away with it all nonetheless. All during the weeks leading up to the hearing, Robb dined with members of the Personnel

-55-

Security Board (analogous to a prosecution attorney sucking up to the judge in a trial) and the lot of them spent days going over mountains of FBI files on Oppie– classified files not available to the defense– and thoroughly establishing a 'get Oppenheimer' mindset.

The hearing itself opened on Monday, 12 April 1954 as scheduled, in Room 2022 of Building T-3, an old building at Sixteenth and Constitution in Washington, D.C. Dr. Gordon Gray called the meeting to order and read Kenneth Nichols' 23 December 1953 letter to Oppenheimer into the record. In turn, Oppenheimer's own letter of 4 March 1954, a long reply to Nichols, was read into the record as well, by Gordon Gray.

The Oppenheimer letter explained that during the 1930s the Depression began to force him to take an interest in the economics of the era, and that his involvement with various left-wing groups at the time had to do with humanitarian causes and not any sympathies with foreign governments. He denied ever being a member of the Communist Party and stressed that his participation in leftist organizations had ceased forever by early 1943 when he went to work at Los Alamos, although he had made an error in judgment in not reporting the Haakon Chevalier incident immediately. He went on to mention– prehaps significantly for our purposes– with regard to the facilities at Los Alamos during the post-war years: "Los Alamos also had wide interests in scientific matters only indirectly related to the weapons program" (Polenberg, 25). (Recall the story of the wreckage from the Aztec retrieval operation being transported to Los Alamos.)

Further, the letter speaks of Oppenheimer's thoughts, over the years, on the H-bomb question, explaining why the General Advisory Committee initially advised against a crash program, and emphasizing: "I never urged anyone not to work on the hydrogen bomb project" (Polenberg, 27).

Gordon Gray advised everyone that if classified information was going to be presented at any time before the board, those not authorized to hear it would be excused for the time being. (This of course would repeatedly occur, and Oppenheimer's attorneys themselves would have to leave the room, since they were not cleared!)

On Tuesday, 13 April Gordon Gray expressed anger that news of the AEC's letter to Oppenheimer had been leaked to the press through James Reston of the *New York Times*; clearly the AEC wanted little or no publicity in the matter. Much of the rest of the day Oppenheimer testified about his position on the H-bomb, pointing out that after Truman ordered a go-ahead in January 1950, the GAC no longer put up any opposition to the program. (All of this would be reiterated many times in many different ways over the coming weeks, to what effect it is difficult to imagine–basically, Oppie's enemies seem to have had their minds made up.)

On Wednesday, 14 April Oppenheimer testified about his younger brother Frank, who was also a physicist and had undeniably been a Communist Party member, though he had left the Party in 1941, well before working at Oak Ridge and (briefly) Los Alamos. Robb cross-examined Oppenheimer at length about communist sympathies in the past. At length Oppie snapped back at him: "Look, I have had a lot of secrets in my head a long time. It does not matter who I associate with. I don't talk about those secrets" (Polenberg, 60). (The "lot of secrets" remark is interesting and suggestive, given those *other* matters Oppie seems to have known about.) It's remarkable, really, that Oppie managed to be so civil to his hostile questioners in these sessions, given that he was sometimes arrogant and snappish in human interactions, and given his intolerance, even in the rarified atmosphere of academia and science, of anything he perceived as stupidity. He probably hadn't ever encountered *real* stupidity until he started dealing with government.

Questions were raised about why, when he finally told security officers about the Haakon Chevalier affair, Oppenheimer had misrepresented things apparently by claiming that Chevalier had approached three different people (a pointless misrepresentation that was to haunt Chevalier for many years), and when Oppenheimer was asked "Why did you do that, Doctor?" he replied, "Because I was an idiot" (Polenberg, 68).

On Thursday, 15 April, in a bizarre string of testimony, General Groves, who originally appointed Oppenheimer to the directorship of Los Alamos, first reaffirmed his view that he had been correct in appointing Oppenheimer, who had done "a magnificent job as far as the war effort was concerned," but later declared, "I would not clear Dr. Oppenheimer today" (Polenberg, 76-81). Actually this apparent contradiction may not be so bizarre when one considers the possible implication: that clearing Oppie in terms of what he knew about in 1954 may not have been the same ball game as having cleared Oppie in 1942 in terms of what he knew then. (Considering the matter of crash retrievals, a lot of water had flowed under the bridge from 1947 on.)

On Friday, 16 April Roger Robb examined Oppenheimer on the subject, again, of the H-bomb, or the 'super' as it was called. Oppenheimer, when asked "Would you have supported the dropping of a thermonuclear bomb on Hiroshima?" replied, "It would have made no sense at all." When asked why not, he said: "The target is too small" (Polenberg, 97). Perpetually in this affair we see that (some) scientists understood, while (most) non-scientists did not, that the H-bomb could never be a tactical weapon, having really no possible purpose but destruction on a stupefyingly huge scale. Interestingly, Oppie during this session referred to "a great deal that happened between '45 and '49– I am not supposed to say to what extent" (Polenberg, 98). (The 1947 and 1948 UFO crash retrievals would certainly account for this remark, especially given his stated inability to go into any detail.)

Further testimony, from John Lansdale, former Los Alamos security officer, brought out an important point that others would later try to make too, with regard to Oppenheimer's erstwhile leftist political enthusiasms: that flirting with communism (lower case) for philosophical reasons in the 1930s or early 1940s and flirting with Communism (upper case) for political reasons in the 1950s were two very different things: "[T]he appraisal or evaluation of associations in the forties must be viewed in the light of the atmosphere existing then and not in the light of the atmosphere existing at the present time" (Polenberg, 119). Given the way things ultimately seem fated to go, this was apparently too subtle a point for political hacks of the day; Lansdale might as well have tried to explain it to the cat. (Possibly a cat might have followed the argument more perceptively.)

On Monday, 19 April Dr. Hans Bette, whom Oppenheimer had appointed head of the theoretical division at Los Alamos, testified in praise of Oppie's leadership in the Manhattan Project, remarking, with regard to security-mindedness, that "many of us did not see sometimes the need for the strictness of the requirements and Dr. Oppenheimer was, I think, considerably more ready to see this need and to enforce security rules" (Polenberg, 129). He also remarked, of Oppenheimer, that "if he differed from other people in his judgment . . . it was because of a deeper thinking about the possible consequences of our actions than the other people had" (Polenberg, 135). How much more perceptively a scientist can often assess the thinking of a fellow scientist!

On Tuesday, 20 April George F. Kennan, former director of the State Department's policy planning staff and ambassador to Russia, testified, when asked about the Chevalier affair, that "in 1943 the Soviet Union was hardly regarded by our top people in our Government as an enemy" (Polenberg, 142) so that the significance of this incident was probably quite overblown. My own point here is that the hearing board had ample reason to know this, and that the Chevalier affair makes a far less cogent reason for deciding against Oppie than his opponents would have had everybody believe. Kennan tried also to explain that there is an inherent paradox in expecting first-rate scientists (whose ways of thinking are often well-nigh incomprehensible to non-scientists) to toe the line in security matters in the same manner as other people. He quoted Addison: "Great wits are near to madness, close allied and thin partitions do their bounds divide," whereupon Oppenheimer, listening nearby, smiled pensively.

The same day, one of the other people to testify was Nobel Prize winning physicist Enrico Fermi, who was asked about the so-called Halloween meeting of the AEC's General Advisory Committee, where the agenda had been to decide what to recommend about development of the H-bomb. Fermi said that "the pressure for this development was extremely inordinate," that "one should try to outlaw the thing before it was born," and that the general concern at the GAC had been to try to "see that the various provisions that were taken for furthering the hydrogen program would not be of such a nature of interfering seriously with the conventional weapons program" (Polenberg, 154). These remarks should have made it clear to the examining board that Oppenheimer had never been a lone, loony voice railing unreasonably (or treasonably) against the development of the H-bomb.

Another witness was David Lilienthal, former chairman of the Atomic Energy Commission, who complained that when (in preparation to testify) he was given the AEC file on Oppenheimer's 1947 security clearance, "vital parts of these records had been removed," and expressed the view, with regard to the Chevalier incident: "[T]he thing that dismissed the concern from my mind was the fact that General Groves and Mr. Lansdale, the security officer . . . were apparently satisfied that this . . . did not endanger the national security" (Polenberg, 156, 160). I.e., if the Chevalier incident wasn't a big deal in 1943, why should it be such a big deal in 1954?

On Wednesday, 21 April Oppenheimer's close friend Isador I. Rabi, the Columbia University physicist who replaced Oppenheimer on the General Advisory Committee, testified that Oppenheimer had in no way pressured anyone on the GAC to oppose the H-bomb program. Further, he remarked that "the suspension of the clearance of Dr. Oppenheimer was a very unfortunate thing that should not have been done" because of Oppenheimer's accomplishments for his country: "We have an A-bomb and a whole series of it . . . and what more do you want, mermaids?" (Polenberg, 178).

On Thursday, 22 April Norris Bradbury, who in 1945 had succeeded Oppenheimer as director of the Los Alamos Scientific Laboratory, testified that his predecessor had more than demonstrated his loyalty to his country. Lee DuBridge, president of the California Institute of Technology, testified that "to question the integrity and loyalty of a person who has worked hard and devotedly for his country as Dr. Oppenheimer has on such trivial grounds is against all principles of human justice" (Polenberg, 191).

On Friday, 23 April a fight on the floor occurred when Oppenheimer's attorney Lloyd Garrison requested that prosecuting attorney Roger Robb provide Garrison's team with the names, in advance, of the witnesses Robb intended to call (a courtesy that Garrison had voluntarily extended to Robb). Robb refused, and Gordon Gray upheld his refusal.

The same day, Dr. Vannevar Bush was called to testify. An eminent figure in science, Bush taught and served as dean at MIT and had served as director of the Office of Scientific Research and Development. Recall, also, that he was a member of Majestic-12 (as was board chairman Gordon Gray, but the difference was that Bush was, to Oppenheimer, a fellow scientist) and had accompanied Oppenheimer on at least one UFO crash retrieval excursion. Significantly, he remarked during his testimony: "I had at the time of the Los Alamos appointment complete confidence in the loyalty, judgment, and integrity of Dr. Oppenheimer. I have certainly no reason to change that opinion in the meantime. I have had plenty of reason to confirm it, for *I worked with him on many occasions on very difficult matters*" (Polenberg, 203, emphasis added). (One wonders if some of those "difficult matters" weren't projects like the Aztec crash retrieval.) Later, after describing in detail his own reservations about the H-bomb, Bush added: "[H]ere is a man who is being pilloried because he had strong opinions, and had the temerity to express them" (Polenberg, 204). With what must have been eye-popping audacity, he went so far as to question the board members' wisdom in even agreeing to sit on such a board, and went on to say that maybe if it was a crime to possess and express opinions, the board should try *him*.

I strongly suspect that he was so passionate on

these points precisely because he knew that the real reasons why government officials were worried about Oppenheimer's access to restricted information had to do not just with nuclear weaponry but with UFO-related secrets as well, and thus saw this whole affair as a criminally disingenuous persecution of a great man. (It must have more than crossed his mind, too, that if Oppenheimer was kicked out of government service and denied access to classified data, he would no longer be available as a valuable resource in any future crash retrievals or similar endeavors.)

On Monday, 26 April Oppie's wife Katherine (Kitty) Oppenheimer testified about her former association with communism. Gordon Gray asked her, "[C]an a distinction be made between the Soviet communism and communism?" Kitty replied: "In the days that I was a member of the Communist Party, I thought they were definitely two things. The Soviet Union had its Communist Party and our country had its Communist Party. I thought that the Communist Party of the United States was concerned with problems internal. I now no longer believe this. I believe the whole thing is linked together and spread all over the world" (Polenberg, 215). Later that day Charles Lauritson, a physicist who had worked with Oppie at Los Alamos, testified that Oppie's interest in communism in the early days had to do not with political systems but with "interest in social causes, a compassion for the underdog," and that "there is a great deal of difference between being a Communist in 1935 and being a Communist in 1954" (Polenberg, 217, 220). As I have mentioned, this point was made over and over by various people during the hearing, but in the end this seemed to make no difference. The real purposes for wanting Oppie out of the loop were, after all, arguably quite different from the ones given. (A covert agenda is a wondrous thing.)

On Tuesday, 27 April the board heard testimony from Dr. John von Neumann, who had originally come to the U.S. from Hungary to teach mathematical physics at Princeton and had been appointed to the Institute for Advanced Study. Robert Sarbacher, remember, said that von Neumann had attended UFO-related meetings at Wright Field in Ohio, meetings at which Sarbacher believed Oppenheimer was also present. Responding to questions about the Chevalier affair, von Neumann remarked that in the early 1940s Oppenheimer, like other scientists, had yet to learn to be emotionally up to dealing with the relation between science and national security, and that such scientists "got suddenly in contact with a universe we had not known before." Of the Chevalier affair he further said: "So if this story is true, that would just give me a piece of information on how long it took Dr. Oppenheimer to get adjusted to this Buck Rogers universe" (Polenberg, 234-35)– an interesting choice of words, all things considered.

On Wednesday, 28 April the board interviewed Dr. Edward Teller, long known as the one man squarely behind the development of the H-bomb. Robb and Rolander had interviewed him a month before the hearing started,and oddly enough he had remarked at that time that Oppenheimer should not lose his security clearance. More recently, Robb had met with him again attempting to change his mind.

During the hearing, Teller remarked: "I would like to see the vital interests of this country in hands which I understand better, and therefore trust more" (Polenberg, 253). After much discussion of Oppenheimer's attitudes toward the thermonuclear weapons program, Gordon Gray asked Teller whether it would endanger national security to restore Oppenheimer's clearance. Teller replied: "To the extent . . . that your question is directed toward intent, I would say I do not see any reason to deny clearance. If it is a question of wisdom and judgment, as demonstrated by actions since 1945, then I would say one would be wiser not to grant clearance" (Polenberg, 264).

When Teller was leaving the room, he paused and held out his hand to Oppenheimer (who took it) and said, "I'm sorry." Oppenheimer replied, "After what you've just said, I don't know what you mean" (Goodchild, 244). A few weeks later when the AEC published the unclassified portions of the hearing transcripts despite having promised Teller and other witnesses that they would not do so, Teller, who had never wanted his rôle in the Oppenheimer matter to be public knowledge, found himself undergoing a kind of ostracism "at the hand of my fellow physicists, akin to the shunning practiced by some religious groups" (Goodchild, 249).

Teller may or may not have known about Oppenheimer's involvement with UFO crash retrieval activities, but he was no stranger to UFO reports himself. Edward Ruppelt, director of the Air Force's Project Blue Book, reported that when the Air Force investigated numerous reports of strange green fireballs over New Mexico in late 1948 and early 1949, at length "a conference was called at Los Alamos to determine what should be done to further pursue the investigation," and that "[s]uch notable scientists as Dr. Joseph Kaplan, a world-renowned authority on the physics of the upper atmosphere, Dr. Edward Teller, of H-bomb fame, and of course Dr. [Lincoln] La Paz, attended, along with a lot of military brass and scientists from Los Alamos" (Ruppelt, 75). But these were only investigations of airborne objects, not crash retrievals, and again it isn't clear whether Teller was aware of the more up-close-and-personal stuff Oppie had been called in on in the late 1940s.

On Thursday, 29 April the board heard testimony from David T. Griggs, at one time chief scientist of the Air Force and a professor of geophysics at UCLA. Griggs was fundamentally hostile to Oppenheimer. Asked about the General Advisory Committee's 'Halloween meeting' in 1949 advising against a crash program to develop the H-bomb, he indicated that in his view this stance could have been disastrous. He said that Oppenheimer was involved in Project Vista "to work for world peace or some such purpose"– he made it sound almost subversive, when in fact it was a study commissioned by the Army and the Air Force in 1951 to study the possibility of adapting smaller nuclear weapons to ground tactical combat. Griggs complained that Oppenheimer and his colleagues "considered that many things were more important than the development of the thermonuclear weapon, specifically the air defense of the continental United States" (Polenberg, 273); this would naturally have been a concern all the more important to Oppenheimer by virtue of his having seen, at Roswell and at Aztec, the sorts of things that might be invading American air space with impunity. But of course Oppenheimer, being in fact a loyal American patriot and a real believer in the proper stewardship of secrets with which one has been entrusted, could say nothing about that in public, or at the hearing.

On Friday, 30 April Luis Alvarez, a Berkeley physics professor who had worked with Ernest Lawrence at the radiation laboratory, continued some testimony begun on the previous day in which he had reported that Oppenheimer had once characterized planned H-bomb tests as likely to fail anyway, even if the development program went forward. On Friday Alvarez described Oppenheimer as not disloyal but as having an inordinate influence over other people's minds; and he expressed the opinion that Oppenheimer showed poor judgment in opposing the all-out H-bomb project because the Russians might well develop one in any case.

Later the same day the board heard from William Borden, whose 7 November 1953 accusatory letter to the FBI had precipitated the whole Oppenheimer affair. After vitriolic exchanges among the attorneys, Borden was allowed to read his original letter into the record. Gordon Gray– whatever his views of Oppenheimer for other reasons– expressed the view that Borden's testimony was not "in any way going to broaden the inquiry of the board." (This seems to have been Gray's polite way of saying that whatever other thoughts one might entertain about Oppenheimer, much of the Borden letter was crap.

Gray, a member of MJ-12 after all, knew that the proceedings really had far other motivations.) Lloyd Garrison remarked that Borden had come "to make accusations of the kind that I don't think belong here" (Polenberg, 300, 303).

As the hearing's final week began on Monday, 3 May, Garrison told the board that over the weekend his legal team had decided against cross-examination of Borden. In retrospect this was probably a tactical mistake, since Borden's accusations were so grossly indefensible that Garrison could have cut him to pieces on the witness stand, and probably should have. In any event Oppenheimer himself took the stand to answer questions about the interviews he had undergone in 1943 with security officers Colonel Boris Pash and John Lansdale about the Chevalier incident. Regarding the question of disengagement from earlier communist involvements, he remarked: "I would not act today as I did in 1943 for a whole lot of reasons" (Polenberg, 317). This is one of those statements that sound more inclusive in their possible nuances when one thinks in terms of Oppenheimer's reported experiences in Roswell and Aztec, and in terms of what he knew because of them that he hadn't known in 1943.

On Tuesday, 4 May the board again heard from Kitty Oppenheimer about her earlier membership in the Communist Party and about her disenchantment with it later.

On Wednesday, 5 May Oppenheimer took the witness stand again to answer questions about two letters written in 1944 to a fellow physicist concerning the development of thermonuclear weapons and seeming to be in favor of them, unlike the position he would take at the GAC in October 1949. There ensued considerable rancor among the defense attorneys, the prosecuting attorneys (what else can one call them, even though the hearing was not supposed to be a trial), and the board, over the fact that Robb's team sprung these letters, one only recently declassified and the other declassified on the spot, without any prior knowledge of them on the part of Garrison's team. It was just another example of the underhanded methods employed at Oppie's expense throughout the proceedings.

The last day of the hearing was Thursday, 6 May. Lloyd Garrison gave his long and eloquent summary of the case for restoring Oppenheimer's clearance, citing the fact that Oppenheimer had kept inviolable all the secrets he held, and pointing out that "[a]fter the war he hope[d] to go back to his academic work, back to physics, but the Government [kept] calling upon him almost continuously for service." Garrison expressed dismay that the Chevalier affair had been dredged up and treated as if it "happened yesterday," and said: "There is more than Dr. Oppenheimer on trial in this room. I use the word 'trial' advisedly. The Government of the United States is here on trial also. Our whole security process is on trial here" (Polenberg, 350-51). He thanked the board members for their consideration. Gordon Gray declared the board in recess, and the hearing was over.

All but the verdict.

7.
Aftermath: Oppie out of the Loop— What's Wrong with this Picture?

The Oppenheimer hearing, though fully three and a half weeks long, came and went without much public awareness, both because no reporters or cameras were allowed in the hearing room and because the time frame of the hearing corresponded almost exactly with that of the much more publicized Army-McCarthy hearings. (I myself remember seeing, at the age of 12, the Army-McCarthy hearings on TV; but so far as I can recall, I heard nothing at the time about the Oppenheimer hearing.) The government of course wanted to do the whole thing as nearly silently as possible— in particular Eisenhower and Strauss wanted to avoid a McCarthy-Oppenheimer encounter, in which Oppie would quite easily have made an idiot out of McCarthy, and probably would himself have emerged unscathed— and indeed the AEC had told the witnesses that the hearing transcripts would not be published. To save their own faces, if nothing else, they no doubt would have made good on this promise, had it not been for an unforeseen problem. One of the AEC commissioners, Eugene Zuckert, left a 241-page summary of the hearing on the D.C. commuter train when he got off in Stamford, Connecticut. Faced with the possibility that someone would find and publish the misplaced document, the

AEC decided to beat everyone to the punch and publish the unclassified portions of the hearing transcripts themselves, though ironically the lost document was recovered safely when the train reached Boston. Some witnesses– especially Edward Teller– had hoped to do their dirty little deeds in private, with no public scrutiny brought to bear at all, but alas for them, it was not to be. The dirty laundry got hung out after all, at least a good portion of it.

But of course the really dirty stuff was the decision that the AEC ultimately reached.

Three weeks after Oppenheimer's hearing ended, the Personnel Security Board chair Gordon Gray and fellow board member Thomas Morgan sent a letter to AEC General Manager Kenneth Nichols stating: "We have . . . been unable to arrive at the conclusion that it would be clearly consistent with the security interests of the United States to reinstate Dr. Oppenheimer's clearance and, therefore, do not so recommend," citing Oppenheimer's "serious disregard for the requirements of the security system," his "susceptibility to influence which could have serious implications for the security interests of the country," his "conduct in the hydrogen-bomb program," and his having been "less than candid in several instances in his testimony before this board." They intimated that better behavior was expected "of one who *has customarily had access to information of the highest classification*" (Polenberg, 361-62, emphasis added). Remember, Dr. Robert Sarbacher, scientific advisor to the U.S. Defense Department's Research and Development Commission, said, of the whole subject of UFOs, that "it is classified two points higher even than the H-bomb. In fact it is the most highly classified subject in the U.S. Government at the present time." So Gordon Gray, in alluding to "information of the highest classification," was referring not only to atomic secrets but to other matters that he, as a member of MJ-12, had reason to know were even *more* secret. And on the basis of *everything he knew* about Oppenheimer, he recommended that his clearance not be restored.

The third member of the board, Ward Evans, dissented from the majority view, writing his own minority report. He pointed out that the AEC had given Oppenheimer a Q-clearance in 1947 already knowing most of the derogatory information about him that had been trotted out at the hearing. (Here he was getting at precisely what is wrong with the logic of the majority decision.) He further said: "He did not hinder the development of the H-bomb and there is absolutely nothing in the testimony to show that he did." And: "I personally think that our failure to clear Dr. Oppenheimer will be a black mark on the escutcheon of our country" (Polenberg, 365).

All of this material went to Kenneth Nichols, who was just supposed to forward it to the AEC, where the commissioners themselves would formally make the final decision like a sort of court of appeals. But instead of doing his job, Nichols wrote up and submitted his own confidential report, substantially changing the reasons for recommending that Oppenheimer's clearance not be reinstated and questioning "his character and veracity in general" (Polenberg, 374). The fact that this report did not flow out of the Personnel Security Board's lengthy hearings, but rather emerged as Nichols' own spin on the question, has to be one of the most outrageous aspects of the whole affair. Again, in a sane world such people would have been prosecuted themselves.

In the end, the judgment of the AEC commissioners was four to one against Oppenheimer: Lewis Strauss, Eugene Zuckert, Joseph Campbell, and Thomas Murray voted to deny clearance, while Henry DeWolf Smyth (significantly, the only scientist among the commissioners) cast the one dissenting vote, favoring Oppenheimer's reinstatement.

Again, some of the wording in the written decisions is intriguing. The main document says, for example: "A Government official *having access to the most sensitive areas of restricted data* and to the innermost details of national war plans and weapons must measure up to exemplary standards of reliability, self-discipline, and trustworthiness. Dr. Oppenheimer has fallen short of acceptable standards" (Polenberg, 380, emphasis added). Once more, "the most sensitive areas of restricted data" is a phrase that takes on added meaning when one remembers that Dr. Sarbacher identified UFO secrecy as precisely the most sensitive data in possession of the U.S. government, and when one notices, in the wording, the reference to "the most sensitve areas of restricted data" *and* details of war plans and weapons– clearly, if this is not simply overblown and amateurish writing, the suggestion is that war plans and weapons are one thing while the *most* sensitive areas are something else.

The main document also refers, with regard to Oppenheimer, to "fundamental defects in his character'" (Polenberg, 380), and one can scarcely resist a smirk in reflecting on the fact that when Lewis Strauss left the AEC in 1959 and President Eisenhower nominated him to become Secretary of Commerce, the Senate turned down his nomination using the same language as that which Strauss had used against Oppie: "defects of character" (McMillan, 259). What would life be, without irony?

Thomas Murray's statement says: "Dr. Oppenheimer occupied a position of paramount importance; his relation to the security interests of the United States was the most intimate possible one" (Polenberg, 388). Every time one sees such superlative description of secrets to which Oppenheimer was privy, one must remember Dr. Sarbacher's revelation: that the innermost, most sensitive, most highly classified secrets concerned not the H-bomb and such things, but government knowledge of unidentified flying objects.

In his dissenting opinion Henry DeWolf Smith interestingly remarks: "With respect to the alleged disregard of the security system, I would suggest that the system itself is nothing to worship. It is a necessary means to an end. Its sole purpose, apart from the prevention of sabotage, is to protect secrets" (Polenberg, 393). He argues eloquently for Oppie, but of course to no avail. In spite of the fact that nothing in the hearing and nothing in the evidence justified such a result, the clearance was denied.

J. Robert Oppenheimer was out of the loop. His government service was a thing of the past.

Outwardly he seemed to take it well enough, embarking on a series of lectures about physics and quantum mechanics and not making reference to his banishment by the government he had so valuably and magnificently served. Inwardly, he was surely devastated. When friends and colleagues would come to call– people still privy to classified data– it was "as though they had been cut off in mid-conversation with Robert" (McMillan, 251). Some of them were moved to tears by his pathos.

He nevertheless returned to his directorship of the Institute for Advanced Study at Princeton, where Lewis Strauss, following him in an undeniably vicious personal vendetta, even there tried in vain to talk the Institute's board of trustees into firing Oppenheimer from that job too. But he would serve as a splendid, if tragic and frustrated, director for the rest of his active life: another thirteen years.

In 1963 President Kennedy invited Oppenheimer to the White House to accept the Fermi Award for physics, given to Edward Teller the previous year and to Hans Bethe the year before that. Oppie, though pleased to receive the award, knew perfectly well that this gesture was essentially a half-assed excuse for an apology, from the government, for the shabby way he had been treated by the country he had served. Indeed there were those who did not favor even such a limited official change of heart toward Oppie. The AEC had been the ones to nominate him (Teller, feeling guilty about his shameful behavior in the whole affair, took part in the nomination), and some people in Congress were displeased. Iowa senator Bourke Hickenlooper went so far as to threaten to introduce legislation reserving for Congress the right to make the choice of Fermi

Award winners. Hickenlooper– basically just a typical politician who clearly had no clue about real science– remarked that he would not attend the award ceremony at the White House because "I have been unable to find convincing evidence of any outstanding contribution to atomic science such as could be attributed to other recipients of the Fermi award that could be credited to Oppenheimer (Stern, *Security on Trial*, 455-56). Sad, that a great man had to suffer such pronouncements from the ignorant. Oppie got the award, anyway, though John Kennedy was assassinated within hours of its announcement in the newspapers, the award being given then by President Lyndon Johnson.

Robert Oppenheimer died of throat cancer on 18 February 1967, a few weeks short of his sixty-third birthday. The Julliard String Quartet played Beethoven's C-sharp Minor Quartet, No. 14, at his funeral, and an era came to an end.

Those of us whom Oppie left behind owe it to him to ask: *Why*, really, did the powers-that-be so desperately want him out of the loop?

One thinks of other, related questions. Why have large portions of the AEC hearing transcripts remained classified for over half a century? What considerations, in terms of what Oppenheimer knew and what it made the government nervous to know that he knew, could justify his being taken out of the picture– no longer allowed access to classified information– in 1954, when he had been cleared to manage the Manhattan Project in 1942-43 and had been Q-cleared anew in 1947? I.e., if his overall demeanor and his complex political nature made high-up government officials sweaty-palmed about his knowing and continuing to learn about classified things, what did he know about in the early 1950s that he hadn't known about in the early 1940s?

My hypothesis, of course, is that given his history of perhaps questionable political leanings (early on, anyway) and his often truculent and rather unpredictable temperament, the government of the United States was a lot more anxious about him by 1954 than they had been in 1943, because in the interim he had been involved in at least two UFO crash retrieval operations of an exceedingly secret nature, and had thus become well aware of his government's involvement in UFO secrecy and cover-ups generally.

We have already looked at the evidence, in terms of research accomplished by people in the field of UFO studies, that Oppie was indeed a part of UFO crash recoveries– in Roswell and in Aztec at any rate, and by inference possibly in other instances by dint of his usefulness and experience in the Roswell and Aztec cases. It remains only to argue that this ultimately was behind the push to take him out of the restricted areas of government service before he could learn even more about things "classified two points higher even than the H-bomb."

But as we have already seen, the logic itself of what happened to Oppenheimer doesn't work until one realizes that there is more than meets the eye. This is always the way with official cover-ups and cover stories– they always suffer from leaky logic.

The primary problem with the logic is of course the problem pointed out again and again at the AEC hearing– that it makes no sense to have cleared Oppie in 1942-43, to have watched him triumphant in the development of the atomic bomb, to have cleared him again in 1947, and then to exile and ostracize him in 1954 by yanking his security clearance. No sense, at least, if one doesn't take into account that he knew things in 1954 *much* more sensitive– as Robert Sarbacher's remarks about classified information would suggest– than he had known before.

If, as some witnesses claimed, the UFO that crashed near Aztec, New Mexico had exhibited an extraordinary propulsion system (as no doubt the Roswell object had too), one may well imagine Oppie's response, his feelings, his probable inclinations and attitudes. What *would* a physicist with his talents, his extraordinary knowledge of energy, think upon seeing a propulsion system that could, according to at least one crash site witness, spell the end of human dependence on oil? Surely any such scientist would naturally and instinctively think: Let's analyze this thing, understand the principles involved, back-engineer the device, put it into mass production, and give the gasoline-burning engine its long-overdue last rites and proper burial. A scientist with Oppie's political influence and persuasiveness (a quality which drew suspicion upon him, much as it had drawn upon Galileo some centuries earlier) might well have pushed for precisely that sort of scenario, and one may envision his doing this in the face of growing opposition, given the extent to which government has always been in bed with the big oil companies. (That he in fact did push the matter in this way is of course a speculation, but not, I think, an unreasonable one.)

We UFO investigators are always being asked why the government keeps covering the whole thing up, and as a matter of fact one could scarcely find a more compelling reason– it appears that if some of the *restricted* knowledge gleaned from UFO crash retrievals were ever to become *common* knowledge, the oil companies would soon be purposeless and obsolete, unless they were willing to make whatever adaptations the situation might require; but corporate giants are typically less than enthusiastic about making drastic adaptations. A lot of money would be at stake. (Let's face it– if there were a cheap and easy energy source, there would be no huge fortunes to be made, and those already making those fortunes would strenuously oppose the change.) If Oppie mixed into this potentially vicious business with the instincts of a scientist and a humanitarian rather than with the instincts of an oil baron or a political lobbyist, he could very well have set himself up for getting hurt. (Never forget the *real* Golden Rule: Those who have the gold make the rules.)

Some basic facts about the circumstances of Oppenheimer's treatment tend to support the hypothesis that the ultimate denial of his clearance had a lot to do with his being privy to UFO secrets– the fact that Robert Cutler (of the Cutler-Twining memo referencing Majestic 12) was present at the meeting with Eisenhower and Strauss, at which it was decided to suspect Oppenheimer's clearance possibly pending a hearing; and the fact that when the AEC's Personnel Security Board convened for the hearing, the chair was none other than MJ-12 member Gordon Gray, who of course would have known everything about Oppenheimer's presence at UFO crash retrieval operations.

Robert Cutler, by the way, remarked in his autobiography that he was "exclusively engaged in the most sensitive matters in government" (Cutler, 318), and again when we see Robert Sarbacher identifying UFO secrecy as precisely that most sensitive area, we realize with added clarity that there were good reasons for Cutler's presence at Eisenhower's meeting. Whether the matter was openly discussed there or not, in front of Lewis Strauss and others present, Eisenhower needed input from someone with a point of view residing at that rarified height.

Further, as we have seen, when one reads the Oppenheimer hearing transcripts already knowing that he was involved in crash retrievals, many things take on enhanced significance, things in some cases not so readily understood otherwise. (Keep in mind that a hypothesis is more authentic the more observable things it helps to explain.) Perhaps the primary example is the impassioned manner in which Vannevar Bush came to Oppenheimer's defense on the witness stand, going so far as to suggest to the board that maybe they should prosecute *him*, if it was a crime to have one's own point of view. Bush, like board chairman Gordon Gray, was a member of MJ-12, but the difference was that Bush was a scientist and Gray was not; both would have been aware of the crash retrievals, but Bush, like Oppie himself, would have thought about them as a scientist thinks about things; the principles of physics inherent in what was found at those retrieval operations would have been paramount in importance, and Bush would have understood, more readily than anyone else involved, that Oppie was going to continue to be needed in the task of comprehending the implications of crash debris. What's more, Bush would have fully understood, and would have seen the matter through a fellow scientist's eyes, that the reasons being given for censuring Oppie– his past political leanings, his fumbling the ball in the Chevalier incident, his reservations (shared by many scientists who were *not* censured for their views) about the H-bomb development– were a façade covering the *deeper* reasons why some people in government felt that it might be uncomfortable for Oppenheimer to continue to have access to some of that 'highest' secret information to which he had been enjoying access. For all we know, Oppie may indeed have been making a fuss in confidential circles about the UFO propulsion systems and insisting that they be emulated and used, in which case Bush, having been at the Aztec retrieval himself, would have known perfectly well that Oppie was being crucified for the sake of oil companies. Or he may have been vocal about the desirability of making the matter of UFO crash recoveries public knowledge, which would have left some people in government and in the military quite desirous of preventing him from learning anything more about those matters than he had already learned.

Gordon Gray, of course, would have known the real reasons for the whole affair too, but in his position he could not have disclosed, in public discourse, those reasons. Some people close to Gray have said that the Oppenheimer matter upset him profoundly. His oldest son, Gordon Gray Jr., talked with him for many hours during the father's last days at Walter Reed Hospital, and felt that his father in the end had "very serious doubts" about the propriety of what had been done to Oppenheimer (McMillan, 228). Much of this lingering dismay could of course be well accounted for if Gray had known, as by our hypothesis here he must have, that the hearing was in large part a sham– that Oppie was pilloried to get him out of the picture for reasons less mentionable than anything the public was aware of.

It is, I think, fascinating that Oppenheimer, who generally said little in public about the matter after the hearing (once simply describing the hearing as a "train wreck"), on one occasion told a reporter that "there was a story behind the story" (Pais, 257). And there certainly was.

One has a sense that, even as impersonal and monolithic as government can be, it should take exceedingly powerful motivation for a government to take the man who had saved the national fate in a world war by developing a theretofore almost unimaginable nuclear weapon, and has thus emerged as a national hero and a resource to be sought out again and again in post-war times by the government itself– it should take uncommonly compelling reasons for that government to come to the conclusion that this same man must, a few years down the road from his time of glory, be taken out of the loop. Somehow the notion of their doing all this on the basis of erstwhile communist associations or doubts about the wisdom of the H-bomb just doesn't wash. It's too much official anxiety, too much reaction for too little reason, if we are to believe (which I don't) that the articulated motives were the real ones. The inexorable historical fact remains– they *did* it to him, and had their real reasons.

It has been remarked: "By taking away the clearance of the man who had replaced Albert Einstein as the public face of scientific genius, the government told the scientists: We want your work, but we don't want you" (McMillan, 262). I would go further. I would go so far as to say that if the government could just have had Oppie's brain in a jar, that would have been fine with them.

My point here, though, is that while nothing can really *excuse* the dump-job done on Oppenheimerr, the hypothesis we have explored here can help *explain* what was done to him. I ask only that the reader consider that hypothesis in terms of the arguments and evidence I have given. Ask yourself: doesn't it all at least make a bit more sense– however unfairly to Oppenheimer– if one thinks of the matter in the light of that hypothesis? Does the hypothesis do a reasonably good job of accounting for what happened? I think it does.

The validity of this argument depends, in part, on the authenticity of the MJ-12 documents, but, as I have indicated, Stanton Friedman and others have done a highly creditable job of authenticating those documents and thus verifying the existence of the Majestic 12 group itself.

An interesting reflection is this: it seems reasonable to suppose that at some point Eisenhower would logically have wanted MJ-12's own input, their own recommendation on whether to reinstate

Oppenheimer's clearance– and what would their vote most likely have been?

As far as supporting Oppenheimer goes, we can pretty well discount the military half of the group, given the military's traditionally proprietary attitudes toward UFO-related secrets. We may note that among the civilians, Gordon Gray would have been unlikely, given the machinations of his Personnel Security Board, to support Oppenheimer; Sidney Souers had expressed negative views on the subject even before the hearings; and Donald Menzel, though a scientist unlike the other two, was essentially a government toady famous for going along with the party line, spirit of scientific inquiry or no. That leaves only Vannevar Bush, Detlev Bronk, Jerome Hunsaker, and Lloyd Berkner as possibly (certainly in the case of Bush) supporting Oppie, both because they were fellow scientists and because they were all with him at the Aztec UFO retrieval. Probably the best Oppie could have hoped for, then, would have been a vote of four for reinstating his clearance, eight against. And even if we have guessed wrong about one or two of the MJ-12 people, five-to-seven or even six-to-six still wouldn't have been good enough.

It appears that Oppie was doomed from the start to be ground up in the heartless processes of government. Undeniably, many others have been, as well, over the years, but few with so brilliant a record of service to those same governmental interests as Robert Oppenheimer.

Coda:
Some Awkward Facts about Government Secrecy and the Law

Whatever else we may say about the Oppenheimer matter, one thing seems quite certain- that when President Eisenhower and the Atomic Energy Commission dropped that opaque wall between Oppenheimer and the world of classified information, they did so with an authority that was apparently not possible to challenge. In effect, they did so with the force of law. Hypothetically, if Oppie had been found perusing a top-secret document a year later- even one he had written himself- he would have been subject to severe criminal penalties. The legal system would have come down on him like the proverbial ton of bricks.

But the interesting question is- what do the terms 'law' and 'legal' mean in this setting? *What is the legal status of government secrecy?*

Here's the surprising thing- arguably, government secrecy *has* no proper legal status, or at any rate not of the sort people think it has.

Let's start looking in the most logical place: the United States Constitution.

Here's what the Constitution has to say about the government's right to keep everything secret: Nothing.

Nothing whatever. Not a damned word.

The only reference, anywhere in the Constitution, to restriction of information at all is found in Article I, Section 5, which says, of the duties of Congress: "Each House shall keep a journal of its proceedings, and from time to time publish the same, excepting such parts as may in their judgement require secrecy. . . ." This is of course a far cry from the wholesale keeping of secrets in the manner in which, and to the extent to which, government has come to keep them, so that for all practical purposes we may say that the Constitution says nothing at all, or at any rate nothing of significance, about the justification of official secrecy generally.

It follows that if the government has any legal basis at all, in the usual sense of the term 'legal,' for withholding UFO-related (or any other) information from the public, the formal justification must lie in *statutory* law subsequent to the Constitution. But here's the astonishing thing– the laws one would expect to be there have never been passed. There is no basis in statutory law for wholesale secret-keeping either. As we shall see, certain legislators have tried, without success, to remedy this situation.

It is significant that when Atomic Energy Commission manager Kenneth Nichols wrote his 23 December 1953 letter to Oppenheimer telling him that the AEC was suspending his clearance, the sole authority he cited as legal justification for this action consisted of Executive Order 9835 and Executive

-87-

Order 10450. Notice that he didn't quote a passage from the Constitution or anything from statutory law, because there was nothing of that sort that he could have quoted. So what is the situation with the legality of such things? Quite simply, executive orders from various presidents have always stood in place of established law. But as one may readily see for oneself, there is nothing in the U.S. Constitution that justifies presidents' issuing executive orders *that function as law*, despite the fact that presidents have done so repeatedly, and despite the fact that violation of these executive orders can carry penalties every bit as severe as penalties for violation of statutory law.

It is instructive to read the Congressional Record for 7 May 1997, to see the efforts of Senators Daniel Patrick Moynihan and Jesse Helms to pass what they hoped to see established as the Government Secrecy Act of 1997. Senator Moynihan, stating that "[s]ecrecy is a form of government regulation," quotes from Max Weber's classic essay *Wirtschaft und Gesellschaft* (Economy and Society) as follows:

> Every bureaucracy seeks to increase the superiority of the professionally informed by keeping their knowledge and intentions secret. Bureaucratic administration always tends to be an administration of 'secret sessions'; in so far as it can, it hides its knowledge and actions from criticism. The pure interest of the bureaucracy in power, however, is efficacious far beyond those areas where purely functional interests make for secrecy. *The concept of the 'official secret' is the specific invention of*

bureaucracy, and nothing is so fanatically defended by the bureaucracy as this attitude, which cannot be substantially defended beyond these specifically qualified areas. [Emphasis added]

Moynihan further states for the record: "[S]ecrecy is the ultimate mode of regulation; the citizen does not even know that he or she is being regulated." The challenge, he says, is clear: "It is time to reexamine the foundations of that security system." He asks a centrally important question– if there have indeed been rules for keeping government secrets, "[w]ere they laws? If not, then what?"

In his presentation in support of the desired Secrecy Act, he points out (and he was certainly in a position to know) that there has never really been any basis *in law* for the official keeping of secrets, hence his effort to set things right and fill the legal void: "The system for classifying and declassifying national security information has been based in regulation, not in statute, and has been governed by six successive Executive orders since 1951." Senator Helms similarly states that the proposed bill "would *for the first time* place in statute the Government system for the classification of information. To date this has been accomplished solely through Executive order."

These two senators' concerns were well founded, in terms of a simple point of Constitutional law: that it is the function of the legislative, not the executive, branch of government– the function of

Congress, not the President– to make law. Oddly, the various presidential executive orders on government secrecy have been functioning not only as law, but as the *only* law, in the absence of legitimately generated statutes dealing with the issue of secrecy.

Naturally, Senators Moynihan and Helms realized– as do all of us who have our heads screwed on right– that in the modern age some information *must* be kept secret. In a world full of terrorists bent on genocide and inspired by halfwit religious fanaticism and kindred forms of lunacy, nobody sane wants vital defense secrets to become common on-the-street knowledge. The senators, in pleading their case for the Secrecy Act, commented: "We must develop a competing culture of openness, fully consistent with our interests in protecting national security, but in which power is no longer derived primarily from one's ability to withhold information." This ideal, they stressed, "requires that secrecy be defined in statute." Further, they warned that the reasons for concealing information could be, in the absence of statutory control, highly questionable.

They argued valiantly and eloquently for their desired law, but in the end their efforts came to very little. By 2000-2001 Congress had agreed only upon a very watered-down and half-hearted Public Information Declassification Act accomplishing little more than to authorize an advisory board on declassification. At the risk of sounding a little paranoid or overly inclined toward conspiracy theories, I would point out that the sorts of deep, dark places in government where UFO secrecy seems to reside could very well not have wanted any really meaningful legislation on secrecy to pass. There surely are persons and agencies– the proverbial 'black budget' sorts of dark corners in government– who can't *afford* to have the process of keeping secrets turned truly 'legal.' Without statutory restrictions, such persons and agencies can get away with a great deal that would be considered illegal in any well-framed statutory basis for secrecy.

As I see it, there is another problem as well.

We live in an age in which it has become well understood that *information* readily qualifies as *property*. Indeed property in the form of information grows more extensive and more universally recognized all the time. Corporations fight tooth-and-nail to protect their proprietary rights to information-based ownership; lawsuits over these matters are practically a daily occurrence. Companies regularly buy and sell marketing information in the form of names, addresses, and email addresses; a company can only sell what it owns, and it can only own property. And when one recalls that the Fifth Amendment to the U.S. Constitution states, "No person shall be . . . deprived of life, liberty, or property, without due process of law," one must reflect upon the notion that informational property falls under the umbrella of the general term 'property' every bit as naturally as the electronic media have come to be included under the First Amendment's term 'the press.'

Following this line of reasoning, we see that the syllogism becomes: (1) One cannot be deprived of property without due process; (2) Some information is property; therefore (3) One cannot be deprived of that information without due process.

Thus, to the extent that one may argue that the public has a natural right to some kinds of information at least, the whole question of the government's depriving people of that information may be regarded as *a due-process issue*. It remains for some history-making test case to establish that notion as legal precedent.

But of course the upshot is– how can arguably unnecessary governmental withholding of information *not* be characterized as depriving the people of property (i.e. of harmless information) 'without due process of law' when there *are* no laws, per se, governing the overall disposition of information on a statutory basis? (There can scarcely be 'due process of law' without *law*.) These questions, one would hope, may someday be answered in such a way as to promote the public good.

Meanwhile, we are left with the sad reflection that the whole question of the legality or illegality of what was done to J. Robert Oppenheimer is mired in the more enigmatic question of what 'legal' even means when one is speaking of government secrecy.

One can judge, nonetheless, that the government's treatment of Oppie was, in any real ethical sense, profoundly and inexcusably *wrong*. A wrong that unfortunately can never be made right.

References and Suggested Reading

Burleson, Donald R. *The Golden Age of UFOs.* Roswell, NM: Black Mesa Press, 2001.

Constitution of the United States. [Any printing]

Cutler, Robert. *No Time for Rest.* Boston: Little, Brown and Company, 1966.

Friedman, Stanton. *Flying Saucers and Science.* Franklin Lake, NJ: New Page Books, 2008.

----------. *Top Secret / Majic.* New York: Marlowe & Company, 1996.

Good, Timothy. *Above Top Secret: The Worldwide UFO Cover-Up.* New York: Quill/William Morrow, 1988.

Goodchild, Peter. *Edward Teller: The Real Dr. Strangelove.* Cambridge: Harvard University Press, 2004.

Hesemann, Michael and Philip Mantle. *Beyond Roswell: The Alien Autopsy Film, Area 51, & the U.S. Government Coverup of UFOs.* New York: Marlowe & Company, 1997.

Isaacson, Walter. *Einstein: His Life and Universe.* New York: Simon & Schuster Paperbacks, 2008.

Jungk, Robert. *Brighter than a Thousand Suns: A Personal History of the Atomic Scientists.* New York: Harcourt Brace Jovanovich, Inc., 1958.

McMillan, Priscilla J. *The Ruin of J. Robert Oppenheimer and the Birth of the Modern Arms Race.* New York: Viking, 2005.

Oppenheimer, J. Robert. *Atom and Void: Essays on Science and Community.* Princeton: Princeton University Press, 1989.

Pais, Abraham. *J. Robert Oppenheimer: A Life.* Oxford/New York: Oxford University Press, 2006.

Polenberg, Richard, ed. *In the Matter of J. Robert Oppenheimer: The Security Clearance Hearing.* Ithaca: Cornell University Press, 2002.

Randle, Kevin D. and Donald R. Schmitt. *The Truth about the UFO Crash at Roswell.* New York: M. Evans and Company, 1994.

Ruppelt, Edward J. *The Report on Unidentified Flying Objects.* New York: Doubleday & Company, 1956.

Steinman, William S. (with contributions by Wendelle C. Stevens). *UFO Crash at Aztec: A Well Kept Secret.* Boulder, CO: American West Publishers, 1986.

Stern, Philip M (foreword). *In the Matter of J. Robert Oppenheimer: Transcript of Hearing before Personnel Security Board and Texts of Principal Documents and Letters.* Cambridge: The MIT Press, 1970, paperback edition 1971. [Reprint of the 1954 Government Printing Office edition, which went out of print almost immediately upon publication.]

---------- (with collaboration of Harold P. Green). *The Oppenheimer Case: Security on Trial.* New York: Harper & Row, 1969.

Stringfield, Leonard H. *Situation Red: The UFO Siege.* New York: Fawcett Crest, 1977.

Wood, Ryan S. *Majic Eyes Only: Earth's Encounters with Extraterrestrial Technology.* Wood Enterprises, 2005.

"I am become death,
the destroyer of worlds."